KNITS TO BE Noticed

Lacy eyelets in unexpected spots...curvy cables all around...zigzag panels up and down. The rich details in these ten terrific sweaters definitely make them knits to be noticed. All the designs are the work of Deborah Newton, who is well known in fashion circles for her finesse with knitwear. "I wanted the sweaters to be fairly easy to knit, but still have interesting details that would make them interesting to make and to wear," she told us. The styles reflect pullovers, cardigans (including Deborah's favorite, a heavy cotton lace hoodie), a turtleneck, a vest, and a bolero—all with abundant patterns that promise pure joy for knitters who love texture and lace!

contents

2   Meet Deborah Newton

4   Classic Lace Pullover

14   Cable and Lace Pullover

24   Basketweave Raglan Pullover

34   Lace Garter Stitch Pullover

42   Lace and Eyelet Vest

50   Lace Bolero

60   Vintage-Feel Cardigan Blouse

72   Lace and Texture Cardigan

86   Hooded Lace Jacket

96   Drawstring Cardigan

107 General Instructions

LEISURE ARTS, INC.
Little Rock, Arkansas

D1411300

EDITORIAL STAFF
MANAGING EDITOR: Susan White Sullivan
SENIOR PREPRESS DIRECTOR: Mark Hawkins
DESIGNER RELATIONS DIRECTOR: Debra Nettles
KNIT & CROCHET PUBLICATIONS DIRECTOR:
   Cheryl Johnson
ART PUBLICATIONS DIRECTOR: Rhonda Shelby
EDITORIAL DIRECTOR: Susan Frantz Wiles
INSTRUCTIONAL/TECHNICAL EDITORS:
   Katie Galucki and Lois J. Long
TECHNICAL EDITOR: Joan Beebe
SENIOR GRAPHIC ARTIST: Lora Puls
GRAPHIC ARTIST: Angela Ormsby Stark
PHOTOGRAPHY MANAGER: Katherine Atchison
PHOTOGRAPHY STYLIST: Cassie Francioni
CONTRIBUTING PHOTOGRAPHER: Jason Masters
STAFF PHOTOGRAPHER: Lloyd Litsey
IMAGING TECHNICIANS: Brian Hall,
   Stephanie Johnson, and Mark R. Potter
PUBLISHING SYSTEMS ADMINISTRATOR:
   Becky Riddle
PUBLISHING SYSTEMS ASSISTANTS: Carrie East,
   Clint Hanson, John Rose, and Janie Wright

BUSINESS STAFF
VICE PRESIDENT AND CHIEF OPERATIONS
   OFFICER: Tom Siebenmorgen
CORPORATE PLANNING AND DEVELOPMENT
   DIRECTOR: Laticia Mull Dittrich
VICE PRESIDENT, SALES AND MARKETING:
   Pam Stebbins
NATIONAL ACCOUNTS DIRECTOR:
   Martha Adams
SALES AND SERVICES DIRECTOR:
   Margaret Reinold
INFORMATION TECHNOLOGY DIRECTOR:
   Hermine Linz
CONTROLLER: Laura Ogle
VICE PRESIDENT, OPERATIONS: Jim Dittrich
COMPTROLLER, OPERATIONS: Rob Thieme
RETAIL CUSTOMER SERVICE MANAGER:
   Stan Raynor
PRINT PRODUCTION MANAGER: Fred F. Pruss

Library of Congress Control Number: 2008925453
ISBN-13: 978-1-60140-798-6
ISBN-10: 1-60140-798-X

meet

As you study each luxurious knit sweater in this collection, you can sense that the designer is surely captivated by intricate details yet truly loves classic simplicity. Now meet Deborah Newton and see how right you are.

"Mixing yarn concepts with fashion and traditional knitting techniques is where I am most myself, where I guess I excel," she responded to our inquiry. "I am, at the root of all this, a good knitter and lover of the ancient craft!

"I love making sweaters—I never run out of ideas, and I never seem to get tired of it. There is always a new yarn, a great button, a new trend, or an old classic that emerges to inspire me!"

She said the sweaters in this book were designed as a group—a variety of sweaters with a focus on knitted lace as a theme. "I wanted the sweaters to be fairly easy to knit, but still have interesting details that would make them interesting to make and to wear," she explained.

"My favorite was the heavy cotton lace hoodie [page 86]. I can picture this one being a useful beach cover-up—or a nice city sweater to dress up a classic outfit. The Drawstring Cardigan [page 96] with the peplum was designed to have a feminine appeal—with a touch of glint in the yarn; whereas the Lace and Texture Cardigan [page 72] was clearly meant to be classic with a twist—in shiny cotton and a fashionable longer length."

Deborah selected the wonderful yarns that the samples are made in, but she emphasizes that any of the sweaters could be made successfully in other yarns. "Just be sure to test a swatch in the pattern stitch first, to see if the gauge is compatible," she said.

Her design process always makes intense use of swatching, charting, and sketching before knitting the final garment. Frequently asking "What if?" along the way, she looks to both classic and unconventional sources for inspiration, plays with fit and shape, and juggles swatches to combine patterns creatively.

Deborah Newton

With Deborah's love of details, it's not surprising to learn how much she also enjoys working part-time in her brother Jason's mapmaking business, Maps for the Classroom.

"It is my nature to like diversity, and my work life reflects that!" she says. "I have two jobs—both very different! We design, publish, market, and sell educational maps for kids. I enjoy talking to teachers, meeting their needs, and helping kids learn more about their world."

A longtime resident of Providence, Rhode Island, Deborah has been a professional knitwear designer since 1980. Her work has appeared in *Vogue Knitting, McCall's Needlework & Crafts, Knitter's Magazine, Threads*, and other major publications.

Deborah's 1992 book by Taunton Press, *Designing Knitwear*, is considered a classic in design circles. The 264-page guide was reprinted in 1998, and reviewers continue to praise its imaginative approach and thorough advice.

More of Deborah's stylish fashions can be found in the 2005 Leisure Arts book, *Options: Sweaters*, available at yarn shops nationwide and online at *TheLeisureBoutique.com*.

During production of *Knits To Be Noticed*, Deborah enthusiastically shared the news that one of her recent designs, a green coat, was on the cover of the Winter issue of *Vogue Knitting*.

"Season after season, I continue to be very fascinated by fashion, both past and present, knits and non-knits," she said. "I love to keep up on new fibers and yarn trends, and find designing with new yarns a real treat. Yet I am also very much influenced by classics. I have always been a fan of vintage clothing, fashion of the past. I am always on the prowl for old magazines and books. I adore movies of the '30s and '40s, and I am often more intent on the clothing than the plot!"

She suspects that her interest in the structure of garments comes from her early adult years working as a costume designer's assistant and making most of her own clothes.

"I learned to knit from my mother before I was old enough to start school," Deborah recalled. "I loved it. It clicked immediately with me." She knitted all through her school years while earning an English degree.

"I love details in knitting, but I guess the rest of my life is pretty simple. Simple apartment, simple clothes, simple food. I do yoga, I swim. I don't drive; I take public transportation and walk a lot. My office on the other hand, is NOT SIMPLE—it is a little, dense, colorful world filled with yarn, books, magazines, garments, photos, swatches, yarns, needles, and a wide variety of buttons."

Deborah's ultimate dream is to do more sweater books of all kinds, geared towards knitters from beginner to expert. "I love knitting," she said, "and it pleases me no end that there are so many who share that love, especially a new young generation with a totally fresh perspective!"

Classic
LACE PULLOVER

Classic is the key word for this design. Its simple, versatile shape is easy to knit and easy to wear—good with jeans or a fancy skirt. The narrow ribbing anchors the edges and lends a modern look.

SIZES

To fit sizes Small{Medium-Large-Extra Large}.
Sample in size Small.

MEASUREMENTS

Finished bust at underarm:

36{38-42-45}"/91.5{96.5-106.5-114.5} cm

Length from back neck to lower edge:

23{23^1/$_2$-24-24^1/$_2$}"/58.5{59.5-61-62} cm

Sleeve width at upper arm:

13{14-15-16}"/33{35.5-38-40.5} cm

Size Note: Instructions are written for size Small with sizes Medium, Large, and Extra Large in braces { }. Instructions will be easier to read if you circle all the numbers pertaining to your size. If only one number is given, it applies to all sizes.

MATERIALS

CLASSIC ELITE "Princess"

(40% Merino Wool, 28% Viscose, 10% Cashmere, 15% Nylon, 7% Angora; 50 grams/150 yards)

Color #3468 (Orange Attitude): 7{8-8-9} balls

Straight knitting needles, sizes 6 (4 mm) **and**

8 (5 mm) **or** sizes needed to obtain gauge

24" (61 cm) Circular knitting needle, size 6 (4 mm)

Stitch markers

Yarn needle

Instructions begin on page 8.

"This sweater was designed to be the most classic of the group," Deborah said. "The yarn is soft and drapey for a blouse-like quality."

GAUGES

Using size 8 needles for all:
Eyelet Pattern: 18 sts and 28 rows = 4"
(10 cm).
Diamond Panel: over 18 sts = 4"
(10 cm).
Take time to save time, check
your gauge.

PATTERN STITCHES

K2, P2 RIB WITH EYELET EDGE:
Multiple of 4 sts plus 2
Eyelet Row: P2, * YO *(Fig. 3d,
page 109)*, K2 tog *(Fig. 7, page 110)*,
P2; rep from * across.
Row 1 (RS): K2, * P2, K2; rep
from * across.
Row 2: P2, * K2, P2; rep from *
across.
Rep Rows 1 and 2 for K2, P2 Rib.

STOCKINETTE STITCH (St st):
Any number of sts
Knit RS rows, purl WS rows.

EYELET PATTERN: Multiple of
8 sts plus 7
Row 1 AND ALL WS ROWS: Purl
across.

Row 2 (RS): Knit across.
Row 4: K2, YO *(Fig. 3a, page 109)*,
[slip 1, K2 tog, PSSO *(Figs. 12a & b,
page 112)*], YO, * K5, YO, slip 1,
K2 tog, PSSO, YO; rep from * across
to last 2 sts, end K2.
Row 6: K3, YO, SSK *(Figs. 11a-c,
page 111)*, * K6, YO, SSK; rep from
* across to last 2 sts, end K2.
Row 8: Knit across.
Row 10: K1, * K5, YO, slip 1,
K2 tog, PSSO, YO; rep from * across
to last 6 sts, end K6.
Row 12: K7, * YO, SSK, K6; rep
from * across.
Rep Rows 1-12 for Eyelet Pattern.

ZIG-ZAG LACE: Multiple of 6 sts
plus 2
Row 1 AND ALL WS ROWS: Purl
across.
Rows 2, 4, and 6: * SSK, K2, YO,
K2; rep from * across to last 2 sts,
end K2.
Rows 8, 10, and 12: K1, * K2, YO,
K2, K2 tog; rep from * across to
last st, end K1.
Rep Rows 1-12 for Zig-Zag Lace.

DIAMOND PANEL: Over 18 sts

Row 1 AND ALL WS ROWS: Purl across.

Row 2 (RS): K6, YO, SSK, K2, YO, SSK, K6.

Row 4: K4, K2 tog, YO, K1, YO, SSK, K2, YO, SSK, K5.

Row 6: K3, K2 tog, YO, K3, YO, SSK, K2, YO, SSK, K4.

Row 8: (K2, K2 tog, YO) twice, K1, YO, SSK, K2, YO, SSK, K3.

Row 10: K1, K2 tog, YO, K2, K2 tog, YO, K3, (YO, SSK, K2) twice.

Row 12: K3, YO, SSK, K2, YO, SSK, YO, K2 tog, YO, K2, K2 tog, YO, K2 tog, K1.

Row 14: K4, YO, SSK, K2, YO, slip 1, K2 tog, PSSO, YO, K2, K2 tog, YO, K3.

Row 16: K5, YO, SSK, K2, YO, SSK, K1, K2 tog, YO, K4.

Rep Rows 1-16 for Diamond Panel.

BACK

With smaller needles,
cast on 94{98-106-114} sts.

Work even in K2, P2 Rib with Eyelet Edge for approximately ¹/₂" (12 mm), decrease 10 sts evenly spaced across last RS row *(see Decreases and Decreasing Evenly Across A Row, page 110)* [by P2 tog *(Fig. 9, page 111)* in P2 ribs] — 84{88-96-104} sts.

Change to larger needles.

Next row, set up patterns (WS): P4{6-2-6} sts (edge sts: keep in St st), PM *(see Markers, page 108)*, work Row 1 of Eyelet Pattern over 15{15-23-23} sts, PM, work Row 1 of Zig-Zag Lace over 14 sts, PM, work Row 1 of Diamond Panel over center 18 sts, PM, work Row 1 of Zig-Zag Lace over 14 sts, PM, work Row 1 of Eyelet Pattern over 15{15-23-23} sts, PM, P4{6-2-6} sts (edge sts: keep in St st).

Work even in patterns as established until piece measures approximately 16" (40.5 cm), end with a WS row.

Shape armholes: Bind off 4 sts at the beginning of the next 2 rows — 76{80-88-96} sts.

Keeping in patterns, decrease one st each end of next 5{5-7-9} RS rows — 66{70-74-78} sts. (Work RS decrease row as follows: K1, SSK, work to last 3 sts, end K2 tog, K1. Work WS rows as established.)

Note: Be sure to work a decrease for each YO made at armhole edge.

Work even until armhole depth measures approximately 7{7¹/₂-8-8¹/₂}"/ 18{19-20.5-21.5} cm, end with a WS row.

Instructions continued on page 10.

Shape shoulders and back neck

(RS): Mark center 16{18-20-22} sts.

Bind off 5{5-6-6} sts, work to marked sts, join a second ball of yarn and bind off center 16{18-20-22} sts, then, working both sides at the same time with separate balls of yarn, bind off 5{5-6-6} sts at the beginning of the next 5{3-3-5} shoulder edges, then 0{6-5-0} sts at the beginning of the next 2 shoulder edges *(see Zeros, page 108)* AND AT THE SAME TIME, bind off from each neck edge 5 sts twice.

FRONT

Work same as for Back until armhole measures approximately 5{5^1/$_2$-6-6^1/$_2$}"/ 12.5{14-15-16.5} cm, end with a WS row.

Shape Front Neckline: Mark center 16{18-20-22} sts.

Next row (RS): Work to center sts, join a second ball of yarn and bind off center 16{18-20-22} sts, work as established to end.

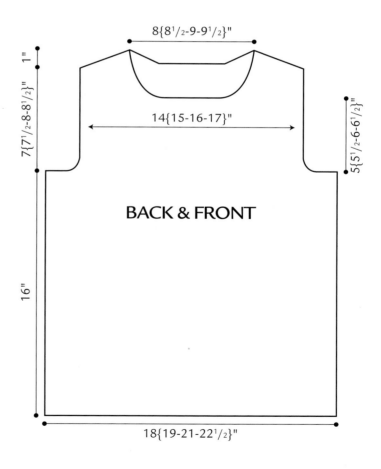

8{8^1/$_2$-9-9^1/$_2$}"

7{7^1/$_2$-8-8^1/$_2$}"   1"

5{5^1/$_2$-6-6^1/$_2$}"

14{15-16-17}"

BACK & FRONT

16"

18{19-21-22^1/$_2$}"

Working both sides with separate balls of yarn, bind off 2 sts from each neck edge 5 times — 15{16-17-18} sts each shoulder AND AT THE SAME TIME, when Front armhole depth measures same as for Back to shoulder, bind off from each shoulder 5{5-6-6} sts 3{2-2-3} times, then 0{6-5-0} sts once.

SLEEVES

With smaller needles, cast on 38{38-38-42} sts.

Work same ribbing as for Back, decrease 3{3-1-3} sts evenly spaced across last RS rib row (by P2 tog in P2 ribs) — 35{35-37-39} sts.

Change to larger needles.

Next row, set up patterns (WS): P2{2-3-4} sts (edge sts: keep in St st), PM, work Row 1 Eyelet Pattern over 31 sts, PM, end P2{2-3-4} (edge sts: keep in St st).

Work 4 more rows as established.

Next row, increase row (RS): K2, make 1 *(Figs. 5a & b, page 110)*, work to last 2 sts, make 1, end K2 — 37{37-39-41} sts.

Working increases into Eyelet Pattern, rep increase row, every 6th row 0{8-12-16} more times, then every 8th row 12{6-3-0} times — 61{65-69-73} sts.

Work even until piece measures approximately 17 1/2" (44.5 cm), end with a WS row.

Cap shaping: Bind off 4 sts at the beginning of the next 2 rows — 53{57-61-65} sts.

Instructions continued on page 12.

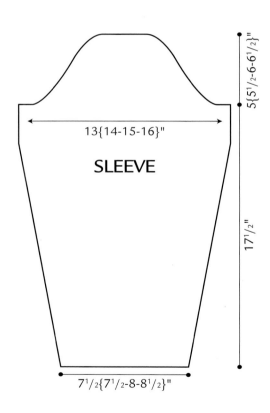

5{5 1/2-6-6 1/2}"

13{14-15-16}"

SLEEVE

17 1/2"

7 1/2{7 1/2-8-8 1/2}"

Keeping in pattern, decrease one st each end of next 15{16-18-20} RS rows — 23{25-25-25} sts. (Work RS decrease row as follows: K1, SSK, work to last 3 sts, end K2 tog, K1. Work WS rows as established.).

Bind off 2 sts at the beginning of the next 4{2-2-2} rows, then 3 sts at the beginning of the next 0{2-2-2} rows — 15 sts.

Bind off remaining sts.

FINISHING

Sew Front to Back at shoulders.

With RS facing and circular needle, beginning at right shoulder seam, pick up 54{56-58-60} sts evenly across Back neck *(Figs. 14a & b, page 112)*, then 74{76-78-80} sts along Front neck — 128{132-136-140} sts. PM for beg of rnd and join.

Rnd 1: * K2, P2; rep from * around.

Rep this rnd until rib measures approximately $1/2$" (12 mm).

Next rnd: * K2, YO *(Fig. 3c, page 109)*, P2 tog; rep from * around.

Bind off on next rnd in rib.

Weave Sleeve seams *(Fig. 15, page 112)*.

Weave side seams.

Sew Sleeve caps into armholes, easing in any fullness.

Cable
AND LACE PULLOVER

A youthful, fun style, this pullover sports lace that takes extra texture from its reverse stockinette stitch background. The twin cables in the center panel draw attention to feminine curves.

SIZES

To fit sizes Small{Medium-Large-Extra Large}.
Sample in size Small.

MEASUREMENTS

Finished bust at underarm:

37{40-44-48}"/94{101.5-112-122} cm

Length from back neck to lower edge:

27^1/$_2${28-28^1/$_2$-29}"/70{71-72.5-73.5} cm

Size Note: Instructions are written for size Small with
sizes Medium, Large, and Extra Large in braces { }.
Instructions will be easier to read if you circle all the
numbers pertaining to your size. If only one number is
given, it applies to all sizes.

MATERIALS

KNIT ONE CROCHET TOO "Wick"

(53% Soy, 47% Polypropylene; 50 grams/120 yards)

Color #141 (Soft Petals): 13{14-16-17} skeins

Straight knitting needles, sizes 8 (5 mm) **and**

9 (5.5 mm) **or** sizes needed to obtain gauge

24" (61 cm) Circular knitting needle, size 8 (5 mm)

Stitch markers

Cable needle (cn)

Yarn needle

Instructions begin on page 18.

"I wanted this garment to be funky and bold, and the lace less traditional than for other sweaters," Deborah said. "I designed the cable by knitting a simple panel with horizontal lace bands, then crossing half of the stitches over the other half at a regular interval."

GAUGES

Using size 9 needles for all:
Textured Eyelet Pattern slightly stretched (using original amount of sts as measure):
17 sts and 24 rows = 4" (10 cm).
Cable Panel: over 12 sts = 2^1/$_2$" (6.25 cm) wide.
Take time to save time, check your gauge.

PATTERN STITCHES

K4, P4 RIB: Multiple of 8 sts plus 10

Row 1 (RS): K3, * P4, K4; rep from * across to last 7 sts, end P4, K3.
Row 2: P3, * K4, P4; rep from * across to last 7 sts, end K4, P3.
Rep these 2 rows for K4, P4 Rib.

TEXTURED EYELET PATTERN: Multiple of 4 sts plus 3

Note: St count does not remain the same. St count increases on Row 4, then returns to original st count after Row 10.
Rows 1 and 3: Knit across.
Row 2 (RS): Purl across.
Row 4: P3, * YO *(Fig. 3d, page 109)*, K1, YO *(Fig. 3c, page 109)*, P3; rep from * across.

Rows 5, 7, and 9: K3, * P3, K3; rep from * across.
Rows 6 and 8: P3, * YO, K3 tog *(Fig. 8, page 111)*, YO, P3; rep from * across.
Row 10: P3, * K3 tog, P3; rep from * across.
Rep Rows 1-10 for Textured Eyelet Pattern.

CABLE PANEL: Over 12 sts

Row 1 AND ALL WS ROWS: P 12.
Rows 2, 6, 10, and 12: K 12.
Row 4: K1, * YO, SSK *(Figs. 11a-c, page 111)*; rep from * 4 more times, K1.
Row 8: K1, * K2 tog *(Fig. 7, page 110)*, YO *(Fig. 3a, page 109)*; rep from * 4 more times, K1.
Row 14: Slip 6 sts to cn and hold in front, K6 from LH needle, then K6 from cn.
Rows 16, 20, 24, 28, 32, and 34: K 12.
Rows 18 and 26: Same as Row 4.
Rows 22 and 30: Same as Row 8.
Row 36: Slip 6 sts to cn and hold in back, K6 from LH needle, then K6 from cn.
Rows 38 and 42: K 12.
Row 40: Same as Row 4.
Row 44: Same as Row 8.
Rep Rows 1-44 for Cable Panel.

STOCKINETTE STITCH (St st):

Any number of sts

Knit RS rows, purl WS rows.

REVERSE STOCKINETTE STITCH (Rev St st):

Any number of sts

Purl RS rows, knit WS rows.

Note: St count does not remain the same. St count increases on Row 4 of Textured Eyelet Pattern, then returns to original st count after Row 10. When counting sts, keep this in mind. All numbers in the instructions are based on original count (Row 1).

BACK

With smaller needles, cast on 98{106-114-122} sts.

Work in K4, P4 Rib for 5" (12.5 cm), decrease 13 sts evenly spaced across last RS row *(see Decreases and Decreasing Evenly Across A Row, page 110)* — 85{93-101-109} sts.

Change to larger needles.

Next row, set up patterns (WS):
P2 (edge sts: keep in St st), PM *(see Markers, page 108)*, work Row 1 of Textured Eyelet Pattern over 23{27-31-35} sts, PM, work Row 1 of Cable Panel over 12 sts, PM, work Row 1 of Textured Eyelet Pattern over center 11 sts, PM, work Row 1 of Cable Panel over 12 sts, PM, work Row 1 of Textured Eyelet Pattern over 23{27-31-35} sts, PM, end P2 (edge sts: keep in St st).

Work even in patterns as established until piece measures approximately 21" (53.5 cm), end with Row 1 of Textured Eyelet Pattern.

Raglan cap shaping: Bind off 4 sts at the beginning of the next 2 rows — 77{85-93-101} sts.

Next row, decrease row (RS): K1, SSK, P4, work to last 7 sts, P4, K2 tog, end K1 — 75{83-91-99} sts.

Next row (WS): P2, K4, work to last 6 sts, end K4, P2. Keeping first and last 6 sts as established, gradually work decreases out of Textured Eyelet Pattern and into Rev St st.

Instructions continued on page 20.

Rep these 2 rows 14{15-17-19} more times, end with a WS row — 47{53-57-61} sts.

Bind off remaining sts .

FRONT

Work same as for Back.

SLEEVES

With smaller needles, cast on 50{50-58-58} sts.

Work in K4, P4 Rib for 4" (10 cm), decrease 4 sts evenly spaced across last RS row — 46{46-54-54} sts.

Change to larger needles.

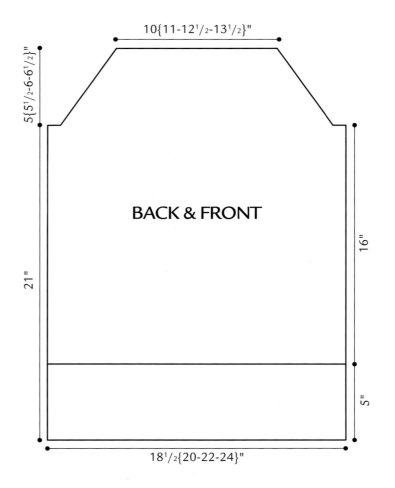

10{11-12½-13½}"

5{5½-6-6½}"

BACK & FRONT

21"

16"

5"

18½{20-22-24}"

Next row, set up patterns (WS): P2 (edge sts: keep in St st), PM, work Row 1 of Textured Eyelet Pattern over 15{15-19-19} sts, PM, work Row 1 of Cable Panel over center 12 sts, PM, work Row 1 of Textured Eyelet Pattern over 15{15-19-19} sts, PM, end P2 (edge sts: keep in St st).

Work even in patterns for 4 rows above rib, end with a WS row.

Next row, increase row (RS): K2, make 1 *(Figs. 5a & b, page 110)*, work to last 2 sts, make 1, end K2 — 48{48-56-56} sts.

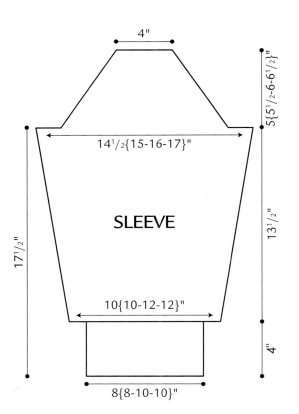

4"

14¹/₂{15-16-17}"

5{5¹/₂-6-6¹/₂}"

SLEEVE

17¹/₂"

13¹/₂"

10{10-12-12}"

4"

8{8-10-10}"

Keeping increases in Rev St st until they can be worked into Textured Eyelet Pattern, rep increase row every 8th row 8{5-7-5} more times, then every 6th row 0{4-0-4} times *(see Zeros, page 108)* — 64{66-70-74} sts.

Work even in patterns until piece measures approximately 17¹/₂" (44.5 cm), end with Row 1 of Textured Eyelet Pattern.

Raglan cap shaping: Bind off 4 sts at the beginning of the next 2 rows — 56{58-62-66} sts.

Next row, decrease row (RS): K1, SSK, P4, work to last 7 sts, P4, K2 tog, end K1 — 54{56-60-64} sts.

Next row (WS): P2, K4, work to last 6 sts, end K4, P2. Keeping first and last 6 sts as established, gradually work decreases out of Textured Eyelet Pattern and into Rev St st.

Rep these 2 rows 14{15-17-19} more times, end with a WS row — 26 sts.

Bind off remaining sts.

Instructions continued on page 22.

FINISHING

Weave Front and Back to Sleeves along raglan shaping *(Fig. 15, page 112)*.

Weave Sleeve and side seams.

Neckline rib: With RS facing and circular needle, beginning at right Back raglan seam, pick up 53{59-59-65} sts evenly across Back neck *(Figs. 14a & b, page 112)*, PM, pick up 29 sts along top of left Sleeve, PM, 53{59-59-65} sts across Front neck, PM, then 29 sts along top of right Sleeve; PM on left needle for beg of rnd and join — 164{176-176-188} sts.

Next 2 rnds, set up rib: [Slip marker, K1 (raglan st), P3, *K3, P3; rep from * around to one st before marker, K1 (raglan st)] 4 times to end.

Next rnd, decrease rnd: [Slip marker, SSK, work to last 2 sts before marker, K2 tog] 4 times to end — 156{168-168-180} sts.

Next rnd: Work in rib as established, (knit the knit sts and purl the purl sts).

Rep the last 2 rnds until rib measures approximately 1$\frac{1}{2}$" (4 cm) or to desired length.

Bind off all sts in rib.

Basketweave RAGLAN PULLOVER

With deep ribbing at the neckline and lower edges, this sweater was designed to be easy to wear. Deborah chose alpaca yarn to give it a luxurious drape.

SIZES

To fit sizes Small{Medium-Large-Extra Large}.
Sample in size Small.

MEASUREMENTS

Finished bust at underarm:

$36\{40^1/_2\text{-}45\text{-}49^1/_2\}$"/$91.5\{103\text{-}114.5\text{-}125.5\}$ cm

Length from back neck:

$22^1/_2\{23^1/_2\text{-}24^1/_2\text{-}25^1/_2\}$"/$57\{59.5\text{-}62\text{-}65\}$ cm

Sleeve width at upper arm:

$13^3/_4\{14^3/_4\text{-}16^1/_2\text{-}17^1/_2\}$"/$35\{37.5\text{-}42\text{-}44.5\}$ cm

Size Note: Instructions are written for size Small with sizes Medium, Large, and Extra Large in braces { }. Instructions will be easier to read if you circle all the numbers pertaining to your size. If only one number is given, it applies to all sizes.

MATERIALS

BERROCO® "Ultra Alpaca™"

(50% Alpaca, 50% Wool; 100 grams/215 yards)
   Color #6209 (Moonshadow): 7{8-9-10} hanks
Straight knitting needles, sizes 6 (4 mm) **and**
   7 (4.5 mm) **or** sizes needed to obtain gauge
16" (40.5 cm) Circular knitting needle,
   size 7 (4.5 mm)
Cable needle (cn)
Stitch markers
Yarn needle

Instructions begin on page 28.

"The traditional cable panel in this sweater is one of my all-time favorites," Deborah said. "It is unusual from a knitter's point of view because the cable 'strands' move, for the most part, by increases and decreases rather than cable crosses!"

GAUGES

Using size 7 needles for all:
Basketweave Pattern:
21 sts and 30 rows = 4" (10 cm).
Lace Cable Panel: over 35 sts = 5¹/₂"
(14 cm) wide.
Take time to save time, check
your gauge.

PATTERN STITCHES

K3, P3 RIB: Multiple of 6 sts plus 3

Row 1 (RS): P3, * K3, P3; rep from *
across.
Row 2: K3, * P3, K3; rep from * across.
Rep these 2 rows for K3, P3 Rib.

BASKETWEAVE PATTERN: Multiple of 6 sts plus 2

Row 1 (RS): Knit across.
Row 2: Purl across.
Rows 3 and 5: K2, * P4, K2; rep from *
across.
Rows 4 and 6: P2, * K4, P2; rep from *
across.
Row 7: Knit across.
Row 8: Purl across.
Rows 9 and 11: P3, * K2, P4; rep from
* across to last 5 sts, end K2, P3.
Rows 10 and 12: K3, * P2, K4; rep
from * across to last 5 sts, end P2, K3.
Rep Rows 1-12 for Basketweave Pattern.

LACE CABLE PANEL: Over 35 sts

C7B: Slip next 4 sts to cn and hold in
back, K3 from LH needle, slip purl st
from cn to LH needle and purl it, then
K3 from cn.
C7F: Slip next 4 sts to cn and hold in
front, K3 from LH needle, slip purl st
from cn to LH needle and purl it, then
K3 from cn.

Row 1 (RS): P1, K1, * YO *(Fig. 3a,
page 109)*, K2, SSK *(Figs. 11a-c,
page 111)*, P7, K2 tog *(Fig. 7,
page 110)*, K2, YO, K1; rep from *
across to last st, end P1.
Row 2: K1, P5, K7, P9, K7, P5, K1.
Row 3: P1, K2, YO, K2, SSK, P5, K2 tog,
K2, YO, K2 tog, YO, K1, YO, K2, SSK,
P5, K2 tog, K2, YO, K2, P1.
Row 4: K1, P6, K5, P 11, K5, P6, K1.
Row 5: P1, * K2 tog, YO, K1, YO, K2,
SSK, P3, K2 tog, K2, YO, K2 tog, YO; rep
from * across to last 2 sts, end K1, P1.
Row 6: K1, P7, K3, P 13, K3, P7, K1.
Row 7: P1, K1, K2 tog, YO, K1, YO, K2,
SSK, P1, K2 tog, K2, YO, (K2 tog, YO) 3
times, K1, YO, K2, SSK, P1, K2 tog, K2,
YO, K2 tog, YO, K2, P1.
Row 8: K1, P8, K1, P 15, K1, P8, K1.
Row 9: P6, C7B, P9, C7B, P6.
Row 10: K6, P3, K1, P3, K9, P3, K1, P3,
K6.
Row 11: P5, K2 tog, K2, YO, K1, YO,
K2, SSK, P7, K2 tog, K2, YO, K1, YO,
K2, SSK, P5.

Row 12: K5, P9, K7, P9, K5.

Row 13: P4, K2 tog, K2, YO, K2 tog, YO, K1, YO, K2, SSK, P5, K2 tog, K2, YO, K2 tog, YO, K1, YO, K2, SSK, P4.

Row 14: K4, P 11, K5, P 11, K4.

Row 15: P3, K2 tog, K2, YO, (K2 tog, YO) 2 times, K1, YO, K2, SSK, P3, K2 tog, K2, YO, (K2 tog, YO) 2 times, K1, YO, K2, SSK, P3.

Row 16: K3, (P 13, K3) 2 times.

Row 17: P2, * K2 tog, K2, YO, (K2 tog, YO) 3 times, K1, YO, K2, SSK, P1; rep from * to last st, end P1.

Row 18: K2, * P 15, K1; rep from * across to last st, end K1.

Row 19: P2, K3, P9, C7F, P9, K3, P2.

Row 20: K2, P3, K9, P3, K1, P3, K9, P3, K2.

Rep Rows 1-20 for Lace Cable Pattern.

STOCKINETTE STITCH (St st):
Any number of sts

Knit RS rows, purl WS rows.

BACK

With smaller needles, cast on 115{127-139-151} sts.

Row 1 (RS): K2 (edge sts: keep in St st), work Row 1 of K3, P3 Rib over center 111{123-135-147} sts, end K2 (edge sts: keep in St st).

Work in K3, P3 Rib for 4" (10 cm), decrease 12 sts on last WS row *(see **Decreases and Decreasing Evenly Across A Row, page 110**)* — 103{115-127-139} sts.

Change to larger needles.

Next row, set up patterns (RS): K2, PM *(see **Markers, page 108**)*, work Row 1 of Basketweave Pattern over 32{38-44-50} sts, PM, work Row 1 of Lace Cable Panel over center 35 sts, PM, work Row 1 of Basketweave Pattern over 32{38-44-50} sts, PM, end K2.

Instructions continued on page 30.

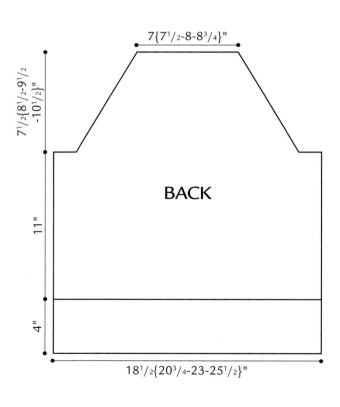

7{7^1/$_2$-8-8^3/$_4$}"

7^1/$_2${8^1/$_2$-9^1/$_2$ -10^1/$_2$}"

BACK

11"

4"

18^1/$_2${20^3/$_4$-23-25^1/$_2$}"

Work even in patterns as established until piece measures approximately 15" (38 cm) from beginning, end with a WS row.

Note: Make note of the pattern row you end on so you can end Sleeve on this same row.

Raglan cap shaping: Bind off 5 sts at the beginning of the next 2 rows, then 2 sts at beginning of next 0{2-4-4} rows *(see Zeros, page 108)* — 93{101-109-121} sts.

Next row, decrease row (RS): K2, SSK, work to last 4 sts, K2 tog, end K2 — 91{99-107-119} sts.

Next row (WS): P3, work to last 3 sts, end P3.

Rep these 2 rows 27{29-32-36} more times, end with a WS row — 37{41-43-47} sts.

Bind off remaining sts.

FRONT

Work same as for Back until 24{26-29-33} decreases have been worked each side above armhole bind offs, end with a WS row — 45{49-51-55} sts.

Bind off remaining sts.

RIGHT SLEEVE

With smaller needles, cast on 67{73-73-79} sts.

Row 1 (RS): K2 (edge sts: keep in St st), work Row 1 of K3, P3 Rib over center 63{69-69-75} sts, end K2 (edge sts: keep in St st).

Work in K3, P3 Rib for 4" (10 cm), decrease 13 sts on last WS row — 54{60-60-66} sts.

Change to larger needles.

Next row, set up pattern (RS): K2, work Row 1 of Basketweave Pattern over 50{56-56-62} sts, end K2.

Work even in pattern as established for 9 more rows, end with a WS row.

Next row, increase row (RS): K2, make 1 *(Figs. 5a & b, page 110)*, work to last 2 sts, make 1, end K2 — 56{62-62-68} sts.

Working increases into Basketweave Pattern, rep increase row, every 10th{10th-8th-8th} row 8{8-4-4} more times, then every 6th row 0{0-8-8} times — 72{78-86-92} sts.

Work even in pattern as established until Sleeve measures approximately 17^1/$_2$" (44.5 cm), end with the same row in the sequence as for Back and Front, if necessary, work longer than 17^1/$_2$" (44.5 cm) rather than shorter.

Raglan cap shaping: Bind off 5 sts at the beginning of the next 2 rows, then 2 sts at the beginning of the next 0{2-4-4} rows — 62{64-68-74} sts.

Row 1, decrease row (RS): K2, SSK, work to last 4 sts, K2 tog, end K2 — 60{62-66-72} sts.

Row 2 (WS): P3, work in pattern as established to last 3 sts, end P3.

Work 2 rows even as established.

Rep these last 4 rows 3{4-5-6} more times, end with a WS row — 54{54-56-60} sts.

Rep Rows 1 and 2 only 16{16-17-19} times, end with a WS row — 22 sts.

Top of raglan shaping: Bind off 2 sts at the beginning of the next RS row, then bind off 4 sts at the beginning of the next 4 RS rows AND AT THE SAME TIME, continue to decrease at the end of every RS row as established 4 more times.

Instructions continued on page 32.

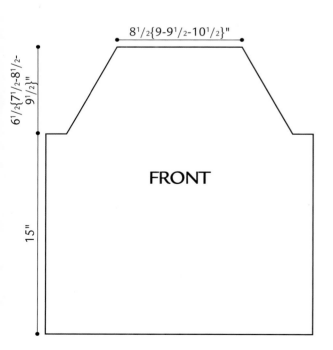

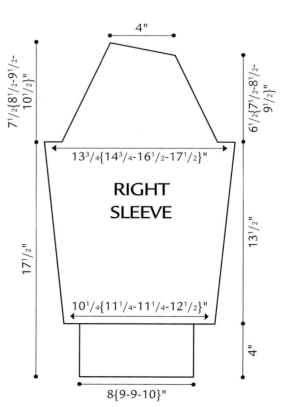

LEFT SLEEVE

Work same as for Right Sleeve to top of raglan shaping.

Top of raglan shaping: Bind off 2 sts at the beginning of the next WS row, then bind off 4 sts at the beginning of the next 4 WS rows AND AT THE SAME TIME, continue to decrease at the beg of every RS row as established 4 more times.

FINISHING

Weave Front and Back to Sleeves along raglan shaping *(Fig. 15, page 112)*.

Weave Sleeve and side seams.

Turtleneck: With RS facing and circular needle, pick up 120{126-132-138} sts evenly spaced around neck edge *(Fig. 14b, page 112)*. PM and join.

Turn so the WS of sweater and RS of collar is facing.

Next rnd: * K3, P3; rep from * around.

Rep last rnd until Turtleneck measures approximately 10" (25.5 cm).

Next rnd: Remove marker, slip first st from RH needle to LH needle, PM, * K2 tog, K1, SSK, YO *(Fig. 3c, page 109)*, P1, YO *(Fig. 3d, page 109)*; rep from * around.

Next rnd: * K3, P3; rep from * around.

Next rnd: * K1, P1, K1, make 1 purl-wise *(Fig. 6, page 110)*; rep from * around — 160{168-176-184} sts.

Next rnd: * K1, P1; rep from * around.

Rep last rnd for 1" (2.5 cm).

Bind off all sts firmly in pattern.

Lace
GARTER STITCH PULLOVER

This easy top is perfect for summer—
airy lace panels let it breathe! The wide
ribbing at the armholes mimics the look
of cool cap sleeves, and the neckline
trim is overlapped at the outer corners for
extra detail.

SIZES

To fit sizes Small{Medium-Large-Extra Large}.
Sample in size Small.

MEASUREMENTS

Finished bust at underarm:

36{38-40-42}"/91.5{96.5-101.5-106.5} cm

Length from back neck:

18{18^1/$_2$-19-19^1/$_2$}"/45.5{47-48.5-49.5} cm

Size Note: Instructions are written for size Small with
sizes Medium, Large, and Extra Large in braces { }.
Instructions will be easier to read if you circle all the
numbers pertaining to your size. If only one number is
given, it applies to all sizes.

MATERIALS

FILATURA Di CROSA
(distributed by Tahki Yarns) "Millefili Fine"
(100% Cotton; 50 grams/136 yards)
  Color #288 (Yellow): 6{6-6-7} balls
Straight knitting needles, sizes 3 (3.25 mm) **and**
  4 (3.5 mm) **or** sizes needed to obtain gauge
Stitch markers
Yarn needle

Instructions begin on page 38.

"I chose a luxury cotton with a soft sheen, but this design would work well in an inexpensive cotton, as well," Deborah said. "Or, knit it in a lightweight wool or lace-weight mohair and you'll have a simple, unique winter vest."

GAUGES

Using size 4 needles for all:

Over Garter st: 22 sts and 36 rows = 4" (10 cm).

Lace Panel: Over 9 sts = 1³/₄" (4.5 cm) wide.

Take time to save time, check your gauge.

PATTERN STITCHES

RIB PATTERN: Multiple of 5 sts plus 3

Row 1 (RS): K3, * P2, K3; rep from * across.

Row 2: P3, * K2, P3; rep from * across.

Rep rows 1 and 2 for Rib Pattern.

GARTER STITCH (Garter st): Any number of sts

Knit every row.

LACE PANEL: Over 9 sts

Row 1 (RS): K3, YO *(Fig. 3a, page 109)*, [slip 1, K2 tog, PSSO *(Figs. 12a & b, page 112)*], YO, K3.

Row 2 AND ALL WS ROWS: P9.

Row 3: K1, K2 tog *(Fig. 7, page 110)*, YO, K3, YO, SSK *(Figs. 11a-c, page 111)*, K1.

Row 5: K2 tog, YO, K5, YO, SSK.

Row 7: K2, YO, SSK, K1, K2 tog, YO, K2.

Row 9: K3, YO, slip 1, K2 tog, PSSO, YO, K3.

Rep Rows 2-9 for Lace Panel.

BACK

With smaller needles, cast on 98{103-108-118} sts.

Work in Rib Pattern for 3" (7.5 cm), decrease 11{10-9-13} sts evenly spaced across last WS rib row *(see Decreases and Decreasing Evenly Across A Row, page 110)* — 87{93-99-105} sts.

Change to larger needles.

Next row, set up patterns (RS): K 17{18-20-22} sts in Garter st, PM *(see Markers, page 108)*, work Row 1 of Lace Panel over 9 sts, PM, [K 13{15-16-17} in Garter st, PM, work Row 1 of Lace Panel over 9 sts, PM] 2 times, end K 17{18-20-22} sts in Garter st.

Work even in patterns as established until piece measures approximately 1¹/₂" (4 cm) above Rib Pattern, end with a WS row.

Next row, increase row (RS): K3, make 1 *(Figs. 5a & b, page 110)*, work as established to last 3 sts, make 1, end K3 — 89{95-101-107} sts.

Keeping in patterns, working increases into Garter st, rep increase row every 1" (2.5 cm), 5 more times, for a total of 6 increases each side — 99{105-111-117} sts.

Work even until piece measures approximately 11" (28 cm), end with a WS row.

Shape armholes: Bind off 6 sts at the beginning of the next 2 rows — 87{93-99-105} sts.

Work even until armhole depth measures approximately 5{5^1/$_2$-6-6^1/$_2$}"/ 12.5{14-15-16.5} cm, end with a WS row.

Shape shoulders and back neck: Mark center 31{33-37-39} sts.

Next row (RS): Work to center marked sts, join a second ball of yarn and bind off center 31{33-37-39} sts, then, working both sides at the same time with separate balls of yarn, bind off from each neck edge 2 sts, 8 times AND AT THE SAME TIME, when armhole measures approximately 7{7^1/$_2$-8-8^1/$_2$}"/18{19-20.5-21.5} cm, bind off from each shoulder 4{5-5-6} sts 3{2-3-2} times, then 0{4-0-5} sts once *(see Zeros, page 108)*.

FRONT

Work same as for Back.

Instructions continued on page 40.

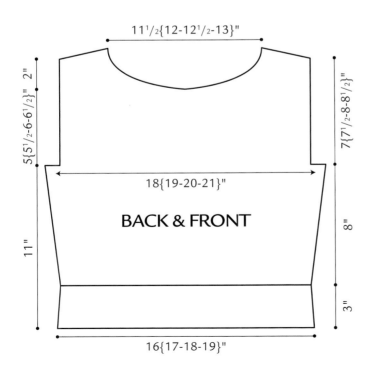

11^1/$_2${12-12^1/$_2$-13}"

5{5^1/$_2$-6-6^1/$_2$}" 2"

7{7^1/$_2$-8-8^1/$_2$}"

18{19-20-21}"

BACK & FRONT

11"

8"

3"

16{17-18-19}"

FINISHING

Sew Front to Back at shoulders.

Armhole ribbing: With smaller needles and RS facing, pick up 103{108-113-118} sts evenly along armhole edge *(Fig. 14a, page 112)*.

Work in Rib Pattern for $2^{1}/_{4}$" (5.5 cm).

Bind off.

Sew 1" (2.5 cm) of Armhole ribbing to bound off edges at underarm.

Weave side seams and remaining Armhole ribbing *(Fig. 15, page 112)*.

Neckline trim: With smaller needles and RS facing, pick up 108{108-113-113} sts evenly along Back neck *(Fig. 14b, page 112)*.

Work in Rib Pattern for $1^{1}/_{2}$"(4 cm).

Bind off.

Rep on Front neck.

Overlap Back Rib over Front Rib at outer corners of neckline and sew in place.

$\mathcal{L}ace$
AND EYELET VEST

This pretty top even has lace in the ribbing!
With flattering eyelet panels in the center,
the vest's round neckline dips low enough
to show off your favorite necklace.

SIZES

To fit sizes Small{Medium-Large-Extra Large}.
Sample in size Small.

MEASUREMENTS

Finished bust at underarm:

36{38-41-43}"/91.5{96.5-104-109} cm

Length from back neck:

21^1/$_2${22-22^1/$_2$-23}"/54.5{56-57-58.5} cm

Size Note: Instructions are written for size Small with
sizes Medium, Large, and Extra Large in braces { }.
Instructions will be easier to read if you circle all the
numbers pertaining to your size. If only one number is
given, it applies to all sizes.

MATERIALS

ARTFUL YARNS/JCA "Serenade"

(70% Pima cotton, 30% Angora;

50 grams/110 yards)

 Color #6002 ("My Funny Valentine" pink):

 6{7-7-8} hanks

Straight knitting needles, sizes 5 (3.75 mm) **and**

 7 (4.5 mm) **or** sizes needed to obtain gauge

16" (40.5 cm) Circular knitting needle,

 size 5 (3.75 mm)

Cable needle (cn)

Stitch markers

Yarn needle

Instructions begin on page 46.

"This vest is so easy to make, and it's meant to be a wardrobe staple," Deborah said. "The yarn has a touch of tweed that gives it a classic edge. If you were to work this design in cotton, it would make a perfect tank top for summer."

GAUGES

Using size 7 needles for all:
Over St st: 20 sts and 26 rows = 4" (10 cm).
Center Cable/Eyelet Panel: over 52 sts = 9¹/₂" (24.25 cm) wide.
Take time to save time, check your gauge.

PATTERN STITCHES

K2, P2 RIB WITH EYELET EDGE:
Multiple of 4 sts plus 2
Eyelet row (WS): P2, * YO *(Fig. 3d, page 109)*, K2 tog *(Fig. 7, page 110)*, P2; rep from * across.
Row 1 (RS): K2, * P2, K2; rep from * across.
Row 2: P2, * K2, P2; rep from * across.
Rep Rows 1 and 2 for K2, P2 Rib.

HORIZONTAL LACE PATTERN:
Multiple of 2 sts
Beginning with a RS knit row, work 17 rows in St st (knit RS rows, purl WS rows), end with a RS knit row.
Row 18: Knit across.
Row 19 (RS): P1, * YO *(Fig. 3b, page 109)*, P2 tog *(Fig. 9, page 111)*; rep from * across to last st, end P1.
Row 20: Knit across.
Rep these 20 rows for Horizontal Lace Pattern.

SEED CABLE: Over 6 sts
Back Cross (BC): Slip 2 sts to cn and hold in back, K2 from LH needle, then K2 from cn.

Row 1 (RS): P2, (K1, P1) 2 times.
Row 2: K2, (P1, K1) 2 times.
Rows 3-10: Rep the last 2 rows 4 more times.
Rows 11 and 13: P1, K4, P1.
Rows 12, 14, 16, and 18: K1, P4, K1.
Row 15: P1, BC, P1.
Row 17: P1, K4, P1.
Row 19: P1, BC, P1.
Row 20: K1, P4, K1.
Rep Rows 1-20 for Seed Cable.

EYELET PANEL: Over 17 sts
Row 1 (RS): P4, K4, YO *(Fig. 3a, page 109)*, K3, SSK *(Figs. 11a-c, page 111)*, P4.
Row 2: K4, P9, K4.
Row 3: P3, K2 tog, K3, YO, K1, YO, K3, SSK, P3.
Row 4: K3, P 11, K3.
Row 5: P2, K2 tog, K3, (YO, K3) 2 times, SSK, P2.
Row 6: K2, P 13, K2.
Row 7: P1, K2 tog, K3, YO, K5, YO, K3, SSK, P1.
Row 8: K1, P 15, K1.
Row 9: K2 tog, K3, YO, K7, YO, K3, SSK.
Row 10: P 17.
Rep Rows 1-10 for Eyelet Panel.

BACK

With smaller needles, cast on 106{110-118-122} sts.

Work even in K2, P2 Ribbing with Eyelet Edge for 3" (7.5 cm), decrease 10 sts evenly spaced across last WS rib row (by K2 tog in K2 ribs) *(see Decreasing Evenly Across A Row, page 110)* — 96{100-108-112} sts.

Change to larger needles.

Next row, set up patterns (RS): Work Row 1 of Horizontal Lace Pattern over 22{24-28-30} sts, PM *(see Markers, page 108)*, work Row 1 of Seed Cable over 6 sts, PM, (work Row 1 of Eyelet Panel over 17 sts, PM, work Row 1 of Seed Cable over 6 sts, PM) twice, work Row 1 of Horizontal Lace Pattern over 22{24-28-30} sts.

Work even in patterns as established, until piece measures approximately 14" (35.5 cm), end with a WS row.

Armhole shaping: Bind off 5 sts at the beginning of the next 2 rows — 86{90-98-102} sts.

Next row, decrease row (RS): K2, SSK, work to last 4 sts, end K2 tog, K2 — 84{88-96-100} sts.

Next row (WS): P4, work to last 4 sts, end P4.

Rep these last 2 rows 4{4-6-5} more times — 76{80-84-90} sts.

Work even until armhole depth measures approximately 7¹/₂{8-8¹/₂-9}"/ 19{20.5-21.5-23} cm, end with a WS row.

Shoulder and back neck shaping: Mark center 24{26-30-32} sts.

Next row (RS): Bind off 5{6-6-6} sts, work to center marked sts, join a second ball of yarn and bind off center 24{26-30-32} sts, work to end.

Instructions continued on page 48.

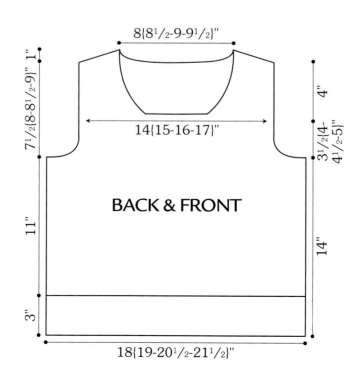

8{8¹/₂-9-9¹/₂}"

7¹/₂{8-8¹/₂-9}" 1"

14{15-16-17}"

4"

3¹/₂{4-4¹/₂-5}"

11"

BACK & FRONT

14"

3"

18{19-20¹/₂-21¹/₂}"

Working both sides at the same time with separate balls of yarn, bind off 5{6-6-6} sts at beginning of next 3 shoulder edges, then 6{5-5-7} sts at beginning of next 2 shoulder edges AND AT THE SAME TIME, bind off 5 sts from each neck edge 2 times.

FRONT

Work same as for Back until armhole measures approximately 3¹/₂{4-4¹/₂-5}"/ 9{10-11.5-12.5} cm, end with a WS row.

Front neck shaping: Mark center 22{24-28-30} sts.

Next row (RS): Work to center marked sts, join a second ball of yarn, bind off center 22{24-28-30} sts, work to end.

Bind off from each neck edge 3 sts once, then 2 sts twice, then 1 st 4 times — 16{17-17-19} sts each side.

Work even until armhole measures same as Back to shoulders, end with a WS row.

Shoulder shaping: Bind off from each shoulder 5{6-6-6} sts twice, then 6{5-5-7} sts once.

FINISHING

Sew Front to Back at shoulders.

Weave sides *(Fig. 15, page 112)*.

Armhole ribbing: With RS facing and circular needle, pick up 92{96-104-108} sts evenly around armhole edge *(Figs. 14a & b, page 112)*. Place marker and join.

Work in rnds of K2, P2 rib for ¹/₂" (12 mm).

Next rnd, eyelet rnd: * K2, YO, P2 tog; rep from * around.

Bind off in rib on next rnd.

Neckline rib: With RS facing and circular needle, beginning at right shoulder seam, pick up 44{46-48-50} sts across back neck, then 72{74-76-78} sts across front — 116{120-124-128} sts. PM and join.

Work rib as for armhole.

Lace BOLERO

A fan of vintage clothing, Deborah took her cue for this design from boleros of the 1940s and '50s. The buttonhole loop closure makes it easy to show off a great button— another fashion element that inspires her.

SIZES

To fit sizes Small{Medium-Large}.
Sample in size Small.

MEASUREMENTS

Finished bust at underarm:
37{41-45}"/94{104-114.5} cm
Length from back neck:
14{15-16$^1/_4$}"/35.5{38-41.5} cm
Sleeve width at upper arm:
17$^1/_2${19$^3/_4$-22}"/44.5{50-56} cm

Size Note: Instructions are written for size Small with sizes Medium and Large in braces { }. Instructions will be easier to read if you circle all the numbers pertaining to your size. If only one number is given, it applies to all sizes.

MATERIALS

REYNOLDS/JCA "Saucy™"
(100% Cotton; 100 grams/185 yards)
   Color #960 (Greek Olive): 4{5-5} balls
Straight knitting needles, sizes 6 (4 mm) **and**
   7 (4.5 mm) **or** sizes needed to obtain gauge
24" (61 cm) Circular knitting needle, size 6 (4 mm)
Stitch markers
1$^1/_2$" (4 cm) Button
Sewing needle and thread
Yarn needle

Instructions begin on page 54.

"This lace bolero is made in one piece—easy to knit and the finishing is minimal," Deborah notes. "It is made from one of my favorite all-over lace patterns that reminds me of swaying underwater seaweed—thus my choice of color!"

GAUGE

Over Lace Pattern using size 7 needles: 17 sts and 28 rows = 4" (10 cm). Take time to save time, check your gauge.

PATTERN STITCHES

LACE PATTERN: Multiple of 10 sts plus 4

Row 1 AND ALL WS ROWS: Purl across.

Row 2: K4, * YO *(Fig. 3a, page 109)*, SSK *(Figs. 11a-c, page 111)*, K1, [K2 tog *(Fig. 7, page 110)*, YO] 2 times, K3; rep from * across.

Row 4: * K3, (YO, SSK) 2 times, K1, K2 tog, YO; rep from * across to last 4 sts, end K4.

Row 6: K2, * (YO, SSK) 3 times, K4; rep from * across to last 2 sts, end YO, SSK.

Row 8: K1, * (YO, SSK) 4 times, K2; rep from * across to last 3 sts, end YO, SSK, K1.

Rows 10, 12, and 14: Rep Rows 6, 4 and 2.

Row 16: K2 tog, YO, * K4, (K2 tog, YO) 3 times; rep from * across to last 2 sts, end K2.

Row 18: K1, K2 tog, YO, * K2, (K2 tog, YO) 4 times; rep from * across to last st, end K1.

Row 20: K2 tog, YO, * K4, (K2 tog, YO) 3 times; rep from * across to last 2 sts, end K2.

Rep Rows 1-20 for Lace Pattern.

STOCKINETTE STITCH (St st): Any number of sts

Knit RS rows, purl WS rows.

Note 1: Body of sweater is worked in 1 piece - from elbow to elbow. Trim and buttonhole loop are worked after the body is complete and after the side seams are joined, Front to Back.

Note 2: To cast on at beginning and/ or end of rows, use the cable cast-on method at the beginning of rows as follows:

With beginning of row facing where sts are to be cast on, insert RH needle between 1st and 2nd sts *(Fig. 1a, page 109)*, pull through a loop and place loop on LH needle *(Fig. 1b, page 109)*; * then insert RH needle between 1st st (newly made loop) on LH needle and next st, pull through another loop and place loop on LH needle; rep from * until desired number of sts are cast on; AND AT THE SAME TIME, after pulling through last loop and before placing it on the LH needle, bring yarn from back to front to separate it from the last loop on LH needle.

BODY PIECE
LEFT SLEEVE

With larger needles, cast on 74{84-94} sts.

Work in Lace Pattern for 29 rows - piece should measure approximately 4¹/₄" (11 cm), end with a WS row.

Next row (RS): Cable cast on 2 sts, K2, PM *(see Markers, page 108)*, work in Lace Pattern to end — 76{86-96} sts.

Next row (WS): Cable cast on 2 sts, P2, PM, purl to marker, P2 — 78{88-98} sts.

Next row: Cable cast on 2 sts, knit to marker, work in Lace Pattern as established to marker, knit across — 80{90-100} sts.

Next row: Cable cast on 2 sts, purl across — 82{92-102} sts.

Note: After casting on, work newly cast on sts in St st, not Lace Pattern. On the last half of the sweater, these same underarm sts will also be worked in St st as they are bound off.

Keeping cast on sts in St st and working Lace Pattern over center 74{84-94} sts, rep the last 2 rows 3 more times, end with a WS row — 94{104-114} sts.

Next row: Cable cast on 10 sts, work across as established — 104{114-124} sts.

Next row: Cable cast on 10 sts, purl across, removing markers — 114{124-134} sts.

PM at each end of last row to mark row.

Work in Lace Pattern over all sts, until piece measures approximately 5{5¹/₂-6}"/ 12.5{14-15} cm from marked row, end with a WS row.

Instructions continued on page 56.

Note: Make note of the pattern row you end on so you can end on Right Front on this same row.

Shape neckline: Next row (RS): Work 54{58-62} sts in Lace Pattern (Back section), join a second ball of yarn and bind off 16 sts (neckline), work in Lace Pattern over 44{50-56} sts (Left Front section) to end.

Work in Lace Pattern, working both sides at the same time with separate balls of yarn, until piece measures approximately 4{4^1/$_2$-5}"/10{11.5-12.5} cm from neckline bind off, end with a WS row.

Create front opening: Next row (RS): Work 54{58-62} sts of Back section, then with second ball of yarn, bind off 44{50-56} sts for Left Front edge.

Cast on 44{50-56} sts for Right Front edge onto empty needle, with RS facing, rep the same RS Lace Pattern row as for the last Back row.

Next row (WS): Purl 44{50-56} sts for Right Front section, then with second ball of yarn purl 54{58-62} sts of Back section.

Working both sections at the same time with separate balls of yarn, each with the same pattern rows, work even until Right Front section measures approximately 4{4^1/$_2$-5}"/10{11.5-12.5} cm, end with a WS row.

Join sections to work RS of body: Next row (RS): Work Back section 54{58-62} sts in Lace Pattern as established, **turn**; with same ball of yarn, cast on 16 sts, cut second ball of yarn, **turn**; with same ball of yarn, continue across the remaining 44{50-56} sts of Right Front — 114{124-134} sts.

Work even for approximately 5{5^1/$_2$-6}"/12.5{14-15} cm, (same row as for Left Front of Body), end with a WS row.

Next row (RS): Bind off 10 sts, work 9 sts in St st, PM, work in Lace Pattern to last 20 sts, PM, work across — 104{114-124} sts.

Next row (WS): Bind off 10 sts, purl across — 94{104-114} sts.

RIGHT SLEEVE

Keeping sts before and after markers in St st, bind off 2 sts at the beginning of the next 10 rows — 74{84-94} sts.

Work even in Lace Pattern for 29 rows.

Bind off all sts loosely in knit.

FINISHING

Sleeve trim: With RS of Left Sleeve facing and smaller needles, pick up 1 st for every cast on st at beginning of Left Sleeve *(Fig. 14b, page 112)*.

Next Row (WS): Knit across.

Next Row (RS): Purl across.

Bind off all sts in knit.

Instructions continued on page 58.

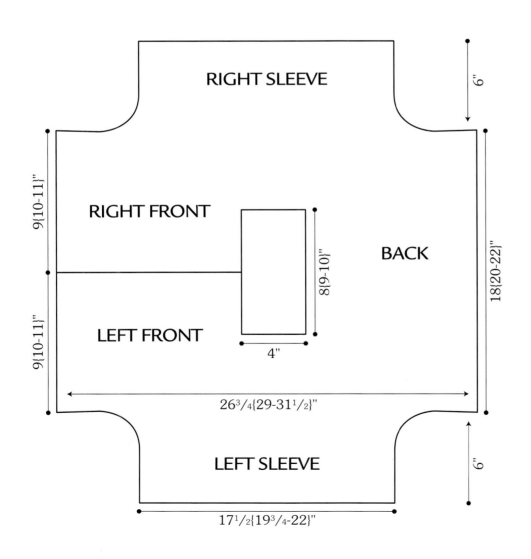

Work same Sleeve trim on final bound off row of Right Sleeve.

Weave Front to Back along underarm and sides *(Fig. 15, page 112)*.

Front and lower edge trim: With RS facing and circular needle, beginning at Left Front neck edge, pick up 1 st for every bound off st along Left Front edge, pick up and mark a corner st, pick up 45{50-55} sts to side seam *(Fig. 14a, page 112)*, pick up 90{100-110} sts along lower Back to side seam, pick up 45{50-55} sts to lower Right Front, pick up and mark a corner st, then pick up 1 st for every cast on st along Right Front edge to beginning of neck shaping — 270{302-334} sts.

Work trim as for Sleeve trim, and at the same time, make 1 st on each side of corners on first WS row *(Figs. 5a & b, page 110)*, and when binding off.

Neckline: With RS facing and circular needle, beginning at Right Front neck edge, cast on 10 sts (buttonhole loop), then pick up 19{22-25} sts along Right Front neck edge, PM, then pick up 16 sts to next corner, PM, pick up 38{44-50} sts along back neck to corner, PM, pick up 16 sts to next corner, PM, then pick up 19{22-25} sts along Left Front neck edge — 118{130-142} sts.

Work trim as for Sleeve trim, and at the same time, K2 tog once in corners on first WS row and when binding off.

Fold buttonhole loop in half and sew to underside of trim.

Sew button opposite buttonhole loop.

Vintage-feel
CARDIGAN BLOUSE

Perhaps because of her early years as a costume designer's assistant, Deborah is fascinated by the structure of garments. This creation is gently shaped at the waistline and rich with details. The lace ribbing gives a dressy feeling at the edges.

SIZES
To fit sizes Small{Medium-Large-Extra Large}.
Sample in size Small.

MEASUREMENTS
Finished bust at underarm:
36{39-42-45}"/91.5{99-106.5-114.5} cm
Length from back neck:
22^1/$_2${23-23^1/$_2$-24}"/57{58.5-59.5-61} cm

Size Note: Instructions are written for size Small with sizes Medium, Large, and Extra Large in braces { }. Instructions will be easier to read if you circle all the numbers pertaining to your size. If only one number is given, it applies to all sizes.

MATERIALS
NASHUA HANDKNITS "June"
(100% Acrylic; 50 grams/120 yards)
  MC: Color #NJUN002 (Ivory): 5{6-6-7} balls
  CC: Color #NJUN003 (Rose): 4{5-5-5} balls
Straight knitting needles, size 5 (3.75 mm) **or** size
  needed to obtain gauge
Stitch markers
Split ring markers
^{1}/$_2$" (12 mm) Buttons - 12
Sewing needle and thread
Yarn needle

Instructions begin on page 64.

Deborah based this summer cardigan on a blouse she saw in a vintage clothing store. "Little pockets, a tiny collar, and lots of buttons! I can picture this worked in a solid color wool, too—no contrast—to wear over a blouse for fall."

GAUGES

Over Lace Pattern: 22 sts and 31 rows = 4" (10 cm).

Take time to save time, check your gauge.

PATTERN STITCHES

EYELET RIB: Multiple of 4 sts plus 2

Rows 1, 3, and 5: K2, * P2, K2; rep from * across.

Row 2 AND ALL WS ROWS: P2, * K2, P2; rep from * across.

Row 7: K2, P2, * YO *(Fig. 3d, page 109)*, SSK *(Figs. 11a-c, page 111)*, P2; rep from * across to last 2 sts, end K2.

Row 8: P2, * K2, P2; rep from * across.

Rep Rows 1-8 for Eyelet Rib.

STOCKINETTE STITCH (St st):

Any number of sts

Knit RS rows, purl WS rows.

LACE PATTERN: Multiple of 20 sts plus 3

Row 1 AND ALL WS ROWS: Purl across.

Rows 2 and 4: Knit across.

Row 6: K3, * SSK, YO *(Fig. 3a, page 109)*, [K1, YO, slip 2, K1, P2SSO *(Figs. 13a & b, page 112)*, YO] 3 times, K1, YO, K2 tog *(Fig. 7, page 110)*, K3; rep from * across.

Rows 8 and 10: K3, * SSK, YO, K5, YO, slip 2, K1, P2SSO, YO, K5, YO, K2 tog, K3; rep from * across.

Row 12: K5, * YO, SSK, K1, K2 tog, YO, K3, YO, SSK, K1, K2 tog, YO, K7; rep from *across to last 5 sts, end last rep K5.

Rows 14, 16, 18, 20, and 22: Rep Rows 6, 8, 10, 12, then Row 6 again.

Rep Rows 1-22 for Lace Pattern.

K1, P1 RIB: odd number of sts

Row 1 (RS): K2, * P1, K1; rep from * across to last 2 sts, end K2.

Row 2: P2, * K1, P1; rep from * across to last 2 sts, end P2.

Rep Rows 1-2 for K1, P1 Rib.

BACK

With CC, cast on 130{134-142-150} sts.

Work in Eyelet Rib for 2¹/₂" (6.5 cm), decrease 25{23-21-21} sts evenly spaced across last WS rib row *(see Decreases and Decreasing Evenly Across A Row, page 110)* — 105{111-121-129} sts.

Cut CC.

Change to MC.

Next row (RS): K 11{14-19-23} sts (edge sts: keep in St st), PM *(see Markers, page 108)*, work Row 2 of Lace Pattern over center 83 sts, PM, K 11{14-19-23} sts (edge sts: keep in St st).

Work even for 7 more rows.

Waist shaping, decrease row (RS):
K2, SSK, work in pattern as established to last 4 sts, end K2 tog, K2 — 103{109-119-127} sts.

Rep decrease row every 6th row 4 more times — 95{101-111-119} sts.

Work even until piece measures approximately 8 1/2" (21.5 cm), end with a RS row.

Waist shaping, increase row (RS):
K2, make 1 *(Figs. 5a & b, page 110)*, work in pattern as established to last 2 sts, make 1, K2 — 97{103-113-121} sts.

Rep increase row every 8th row 4 more times — 105{111-121-129} sts.

Work even until piece measures approximately 15" (38 cm), end with a WS row.

Instructions continued on page 66.

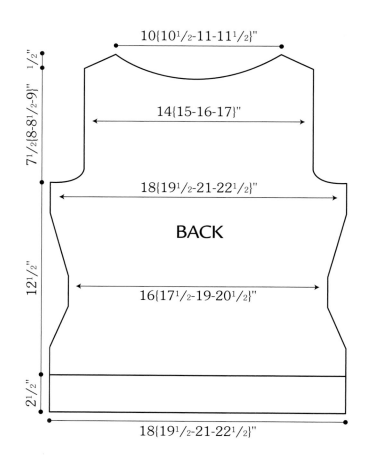

Shape armholes, next row (RS):

Bind off 6 sts at the beginning of the next 2 rows, then decrease 1 st each end of every RS row 7{8-10-11} times — 79{83-89-95} sts.

Work even until armhole depth measures approximately 7{7^1/$_2$-8-8^1/$_2$}"/ 18{19-20.5-21.5} cm, end with a WS row.

Shape shoulders and back neck:

Mark center 25{27-29-31} sts.

Next row (RS): Work to center marked sts, join a second ball of yarn and bind off center 25{27-29-31} sts, then, working both sides at the same time with separate balls of yarn, bind off from each neck edge 5 sts three times AND AT THE SAME TIME, when armhole depth measures approximately 7^1/$_2${8-8^1/$_2$-9}"/ 19{20.5-21.5-23} cm end with a WS row, bind off from each shoulder edge 4{5-5-5} sts 3{1-3-1} time(s), then 0{4-0-6} sts twice *(see Zeros, page 108)*.

LEFT FRONT

With CC, cast on 66{70-74-78} sts.

Work in Eyelet Rib for 2^1/$_2$" (6.5 cm), decrease 12{13-12-12} sts evenly spaced across last WS rib row — 54{57-62-66} sts.

Cut CC.

Change to MC.

Next row (RS): K 11{14-19-23} sts (edge sts: keep in St st), PM, work Row 2 of Lace Pattern over last 43 sts.

Work even for 7 more rows.

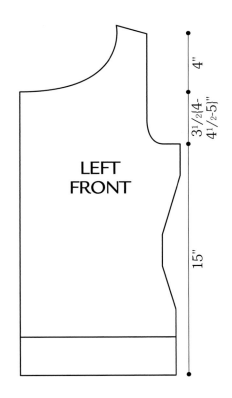

LEFT FRONT

4"

3^1/$_2${4-4^1/$_2$-5}"

15"

Waist shaping, decrease row (RS):
K2, SSK, work as established to end —
53{56-61-65} sts.

Rep decrease row every 6th row 4 more
times — 49{52-57-61} sts.

Work even until piece measures
approximately 8 1/2" (21.5 cm), end with
a WS row.

Waist shaping, increase row (RS):
K2, make 1, work as established to end —
50{53-58-62} sts.

Rep increase row every 8th row 4 more
times — 54{57-62-66} sts.

Work even until piece measures
approximately 15" (38 cm), end with a
WS row.

Shape armholes, next row (RS):
Bind off 6 sts at the beginning of the
next row, then decrease 1 st at beginning
of every RS row 7{8-10-11} times —
41{43-46-49} sts.

Work even until armhole depth
measures approximately 3 1/2{4-4 1/2-5}"/
9{10-11.5-12.5} cm, end with a RS row.

Shape neck (WS): Bind off at neck
edge 6 sts once, 3 sts 1{2-3-4} time(s),
then 2 sts 10{9-8-7} times AND AT THE
SAME TIME, work until armhole depth
measures same as Back to shoulder, end
with a WS row — 12{13-15-17} sts.

Shape shoulders (RS): Bind off at
beginning of RS rows, 4{5-5-5} sts
3{1-3-1} time(s), then 0{4-0-6} sts twice.

RIGHT FRONT
With CC, cast on 66{70-74-78} sts.

Work in Eyelet Rib for 2 1/2" (6.5 cm),
decrease 12{13-12-12} sts evenly spaced
across last WS rib row — 54{57-62-66} sts.

Cut CC.

Change to MC.

Next row (RS): Work Row 2 of Lace
Pattern over first 43 sts, PM,
K 11{14-19-23} sts (edge sts: keep in
St st).

Work even for 7 more rows.

Instructions continued on page 68.

Waist shaping, decrease row (RS):
Work as established to last 4 sts, K2 tog, K2 — 53{56-61-65} sts.

Rep decrease row every 6th row 4 more times — 49{52-57-61} sts.

Work even until piece measures approximately 8¹/₂" (21.5 cm), end with a WS row.

Waist shaping, increase row (RS):
Work as established to last 2 sts, make 1, K2 — 50{53-58-62} sts.

Rep increase row every 8th row 4 more times — 54{57-62-66} sts.

Work even until piece measures approximately 15" (38 cm), end with a RS row.

Shape armholes, next row (WS):
Bind off 6 sts at the beginning of the next row, then decrease 1 st at beginning of every WS row 7{8-10-11} times — 41{43-46-49} sts.

Work even until armhole depth measures approximately 3¹/₂{4-4¹/₂-5}"/ 9{10-11.5-12.5} cm, end with a WS row.

Shape neck (RS): Bind off at neck edge 6 sts once, 3 sts 1{2-3-4} time(s), then 2 sts 10{9-8-7} times AND AT THE SAME TIME, work until armhole depth measures same as Back to shoulder, end with a RS row — 12{13-15-17} sts.

Shape shoulders (WS): Bind off at beginning of WS rows, 4{5-5-5} sts 3{1-3-1} time(s), then 0{4-0-6} sts twice.

SLEEVES

With CC, cast on 78{86-94-98} sts.

Work in Eyelet Rib for 5^1/$_2$" (14 cm), end with a WS row.

Cap shaping, next 2 rows: Bind off 6 sts at the beginning of the next 2 rows — 66{74-82-86} sts.

Next row, decrease row (RS): K1, SSK, work as established to last 3 sts, end K2 tog, K1 — 64{72-80-84} sts.

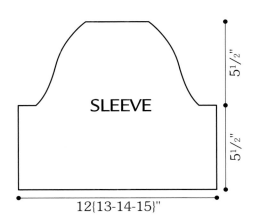

SLEEVE

5^1/$_2$"

5^1/$_2$"

12{13-14-15}"

Next row (WS): P2, work in pattern as established to last 2 sts, end P2.

Rep these 2 rows 18{20-19-21} more times — 28{32-42-42} sts.

Bind off 2 sts at the beginning of the next 2{4-6-6} rows, then 0{0-3-3} sts at beginning of next 2 rows — 24 sts.

Bind off remaining sts.

FINISHING

Sew Fronts to Back at shoulders.

Neckline trim: With RS facing and CC, pick up 166{170-174-178} sts evenly around entire neck edge *(Figs. 14a & b, page 112)*.

Work in Eyelet Rib for approximately 2^1/$_4$" (5 cm), bind off on last RS row.

Left Front Band: With RS facing and CC, pick up 107{109-113-115} sts evenly along Left Front edge.

Instructions continued on page 70.

Next row (WS): P2, K1, * P1, K1; rep from * across to last 2 sts, end P2.

Next Row (RS): K2, P1, * K1, P1; rep from * across to last 2 sts, end K2.

Rep these last 2 rows for $^1/_2$" (12 mm), bind off in rib on last row.

Sew 10 buttons evenly spaced to Left Front Band.

Right Front Band: With RS facing and CC, pick up 107{109-113-115} sts evenly along Right Front edge.

Next row (WS): P2, K1, * P1, K1; rep from * across to last 2 sts, end P2.

Next row (RS): Work 10 buttonholes opposite buttons on Left Front by YO, K2 tog.

Complete as for Left Front Band.

Weave sides *(Fig. 15, page 112)*.

Weave Sleeve seams.

Sew Sleeve caps into armholes, easing in any fullness.

Pockets: Measure 1" (2.5 cm) up from bottom rib on Left Front, and 2" (5 cm) over from center front rib, split ring marker. Measure over 4" (10 cm) from this point toward side seam, split ring marker.

With RS facing and CC, pick up 34 sts between markers *(Fig. A)* and work in Eyelet Rib for approximately 4$^1/_4$" (11 cm), end with Row 2 of pattern.

Fig. A

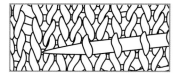

Bind off all sts in pattern.

Sew sides of Pocket to sweater.

Work second Pocket on Right Front.

Sew button to each Front to match center Pocket eyelet, which acts as a buttonhole.

Lace
AND TEXTURE CARDIGAN

A classic cardigan with a twist, this sweater has a long, lean profile that looks good on everyone. Deborah chose a shiny, colorful yarn this time, but she suggests a wool tweed if you want a more traditional Brit-classic look.

SIZES
To fit sizes Small{Medium-Large-Extra Large}.
Sample in size Small.

MEASUREMENTS
Finished bust at underarm:
41{44-47-50}"/104{112-119.5-127} cm
Length from back neck to lower edge:
approximately 30{30-35-35}"/76{76-89-89} cm
Sleeve width at upper arm:
13^1/$_2${14^1/$_2$-15-16}"/34.5{37-38-40.5} cm

Size Note: Instructions are written for size Small with
sizes Medium, Large, and Extra Large in braces { }.
Instructions will be easier to read if you circle all the
numbers pertaining to your size. If only one number is
given, it applies to all sizes.

MATERIALS
CLASSIC ELITE "Provence"
(100% Cotton; 100 grams/205 yards)
    Color #2681 (Bright Chartreuse):
    9{9-11-11} hanks
Straight knitting needles, sizes 5 (3.75 mm) **and**
    6 (4 mm) **or** sizes needed to obtain gauge
^{3}/$_4$" (19 mm) Buttons - 7
Sewing needle and thread
Yarn needle

Instructions begin on page 76.

One of Deborah's favorite details in this cardigan is the texture in the lace panel. "I discovered this old pattern in a book about traditional knitted coverlets; now it has met a new century and a new look!"

GAUGES

Using size 6 needles for all:
Over Lace Column Pattern:
20 sts and 28 rows = 4" (10 cm).
Over Lace Diamond/Cable Panels:
23 sts and 28 rows = 4" (10 cm).
Take time to save time, check your gauge.

PATTERN STITCHES
STOCKINETTE STITCH (St st):
Any number of sts
Knit RS rows, purl WS rows.

LACE COLUMN PATTERN: Multiple of 10 sts plus 2
Row 1 (RS): K2, * YO *(Fig. 3a, page 109)*, K2 tog *(Fig. 7, page 110)*, K4, SSK *(Figs. 11a-c, page 111)*, YO, K2; rep from * across.
Row 2: Purl across.
Rep Rows 1 and 2 for Lace Column Pattern.

CABLE PANEL: Over 10 sts
Row 1 (RS): P2, * K2 tog but do not drop from LH needle; knit the first st again and slip both together from needle; rep from * 2 more times, end P2.
Row 2: K2, P6, K2.
Row 3: P2, K1, * K2 tog and knit first st again as in Row 2; rep from *once more, end K1, P2.
Row 4: K2, P6, K2.
Rep Rows 1-4 for Cable Panel.

LACE DIAMOND PANEL: Over 24 sts
Note: Panel begins with 24 sts, but st count reduces to 23 sts on Row 1 and does not resume the 24 st count again until Row 36.

Row 1 (RS): K 10, K2 tog, YO, SSK, K 10 — 23 sts.
Row 2: P 23.
Row 3: K9, K2 tog, YO, K1, YO, SSK, K9.
Row 4: P 10, K1, P1, K1, P 10.
Row 5: K8, K2 tog, YO *(Fig. 3c, page 109)*, P1, K1, P1, YO *(Fig. 3d, page 109)*, SSK, K8.
Row 6: P 10, K1, P1, K1, P 10.
Row 7: K7, K2 tog, YO, K1, (P1, K1) 2 times, YO, SSK, K7.
Row 8: P8, K1, (P1, K1) 3 times, P8.
Row 9: K6, K2 tog, YO, P1, (K1, P1) 3 times, YO, SSK, K6.
Row 10: P8, K1, (P1, K1) 3 times, P8.
Row 11: K5, K2 tog, YO, K1, (P1, K1) 4 times, YO, SSK, K5.
Row 12: P6, (K1, P1) 5 times, K1, P6.
Row 13: K4, K2 tog, YO, P1, (K1, P1) 5 times, YO, SSK, K4.
Row 14: P6, K1, (P1, K1) 5 times, P6.
Row 15: K3, K2 tog, YO, K1, (P1, K1) 6 times, YO, SSK, K3.
Row 16: P4, K1, (P1, K1) 7 times, P4.
Row 17: K2, K2 tog, YO, P1, (K1, P1) 7 times, YO, SSK, K2.
Row 18: P4, K1, (P1, K1) 7 times, P4.
Row 19: K2, YO, SSK, K1, (P1, K1) 7 times, K2 tog, YO, K2.

Row 20: P4, K1, (P1, K1) 7 times, P4.

Row 21: K3, YO, SSK, P1, (K1, P1) 6 times, K2 tog, YO, K3.

Row 22: P6, K1, (P1, K1) 5 times, P6.

Row 23: K4, YO, SSK, K1, (P1, K1) 5 times, K2 tog, YO, K4.

Row 24: P6, K1, (P1, K1) 5 times, P6.

Row 25: K5, YO, SSK, P1, (K1, P1) 4 times, K2 tog, YO, K5.

Row 26: P8, K1, (P1, K1) 3 times, P8.

Row 27: K6, YO, SSK, K1, (P1, K1) 3 times, K2 tog, YO, K6.

Row 28: P8, K1, (P1, K1) 3 times, P8.

Row 29: K7, YO, SSK, P1, (K1, P1) 2 times, K2 tog, YO, K7.

Row 30: P 10, K1, P1, K1, P 10.

Row 31: K8, YO, SSK, K1, P1, K1, K2 tog, YO, K8.

Row 32: P 10, K1, P1, K1, P 10.

Row 33: K9, YO, SSK, P1, K2 tog, YO, K9.

Row 34: P 23.

Row 35: K 10, YO, [slip 1, K2 tog, PSSO *(Figs. 12a & b, page 112)*], YO, K 10.

Row 36: P 11, make 1 [lift the loop at the base of the next st *(Fig. A)* and place on LH needle, then P1 tbl into it *(Fig. B)*], P 12 — 24 sts.

Fig. A   **Fig. B**

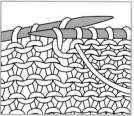   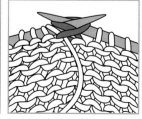

Row 37: K 24.

Row 38: P 24.

Rep Rows 1-38 for Lace Diamond Panel.

BACK

With smaller needles, cast on 129{137-145-153} sts.

Row 1 (RS): K2, P1, * K1, P1; rep from * across to last 2 sts, end K2.

Row 2: P2, K1, * P1, K1; rep from * across to last 2 sts, end P2.

Rep these last 2 rows once more, increase 1 st on last WS row *(Figs. 4a & b, page 110)*— 130{138-146-154} sts.

Next row (RS): K2, * P2, K2; rep from * across.

Next row: P2, * K2, P2; rep from * across.

Rep these last 2 rows until piece measures approximately 1¹/₂" (4 cm), end with a RS row.

Next row (WS): Purl across, decrease 12 sts evenly spaced *(see Decreases and Decreasing Evenly Across A Row, page 110)* — 118{126-134-142} sts.

Instructions continued on page 78.

Change to larger needles.

Next row, set up patterns (RS):
K 0{4-8-2} (edge sts: keep in St st)
(see Zeros, page 108), PM *(see Markers, page 108)*, work
Row 1 of Lace Column Pattern over 12{12-12-22} sts, PM, work Row 1 of Cable Panel over 10 sts, PM, work Row 1 of Lace Diamond Panel over 24 sts, PM, work Row 1 of Cable Panel over 10 sts, PM, K2, P2, K2, PM, work Row 1 of Cable Panel over 10 sts, PM, work Row 1 of Lace Diamond Panel over 24 sts, PM, work Row 1 of Cable Panel over 10 sts, PM, work Row 1 of Lace Column Pattern over 12{12-12-22} sts, end K 0{4-8-2} sts (edge sts: keep in St st) — 116{124-132-140} sts.

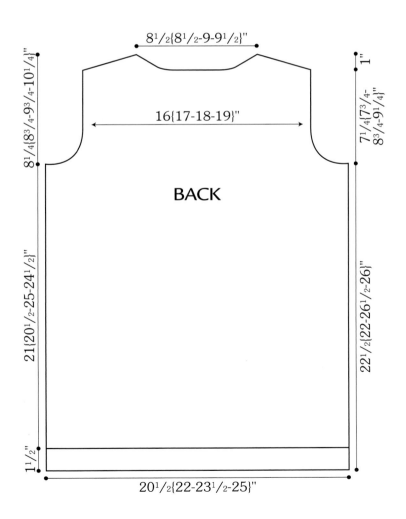

$8^1/_2\{8^1/_2\text{-}9\text{-}9^1/_2\}$"

$8^1/_4\{8^3/_4\text{-}9^3/_4\text{-}10^1/_4\}$"

1"

$7^1/_4\{7^3/_4\text{-}8^3/_4\text{-}9^1/_4\}$"

16{17-18-19}"

BACK

$21\{20^1/_2\text{-}25\text{-}24^1/_2\}$"

$22^1/_2\{22\text{-}26^1/_2\text{-}26\}$"

$1^1/_2$"

$20^1/_2\{22\text{-}23^1/_2\text{-}25\}$"

Note: When counting sts, there will be 2 extra sts on Rows 36-38 of Lace Diamond Panel.

Next row (WS): Work Row 2 of all patterns to center 6 sts, slip marker, P2, K2, P2, slip marker, work Row 2 of all patterns to end.

Work even as established until 146{142-176-174} rows above rib have been completed, end with WS Row 32{28-24-22} of 4th{4th-5th-5th} rep of Lace Diamond Panel — piece should measure approximately 22$\frac{1}{2}${22-26$\frac{1}{2}$-26}"/57{56-67.5-66} cm.

Armhole shaping (RS): Bind off 5 sts at the beginning of the next 2 rows — 106{114-122-130} sts.

Keeping in patterns as established, decrease 1 st at each end of the next 6{9-10-12} RS rows — 94{96-102-106} sts.

Work even as established until armhole depth measures approximately 7$\frac{1}{4}${7$\frac{3}{4}$-8$\frac{3}{4}$-9$\frac{1}{4}$}"/18.5{19.5-22-23.5} cm, end with WS Row 8 of 6th{6th-7th-7th} rep of Lace Diamond Panel.

Shoulder and back neck shaping:
Mark center 28{28-30-32} sts.

Next row (RS): Keeping in patterns, bind off 8{8-9-9} sts, work to marked sts, join a second ball of yarn, bind off center 28{28-30-32} sts, work to end.

Working both sides at the same time with separate balls of yarn, bind off 8{8-9-9} sts from the next 3{5-3-5} shoulder edges, then 7{0-8-0} sts at beginning of next 2 shoulder edges AND AT THE SAME TIME bind off 5 sts from each neck edge 2 times.

LEFT FRONT

With smaller needles, cast on 65{69-73-77} sts.

Row 1 (RS): K2, P1, * K1, P1; rep from * across to last 2 sts, end K2.

Row 2: P2, K1, * P1, K1; rep from * across to last 2 sts, end P2.

Rep these last 2 rows once more, increase 1 st on last WS row — 66{70-74-78} sts.

Instructions continued on page 80.

Next row (RS): K2, * P2, K2; rep from * across.

Next row: P2, * K2, P2; rep from * across.

Rep these last 2 rows until piece measures same as for Back, end with a RS row.

Next row (WS): Purl across, decrease 8 sts evenly spaced — 58{62-66-70} sts.

Change to larger needles.

Next row, set up patterns: (RS): K 0{4-8-2} (edge sts: keep in St st), PM, work Row 1 of Lace Column Pattern over 12{12-12-22} sts, PM, work Row 1 of Cable Panel over 10 sts, PM, work Row 1 of Lace Diamond Panel over 24 sts, PM, work Row 1 of Cable Panel over 10 sts, PM, K2 (edge sts: keep in St st) — 57{61-65-69} sts.

Note: When counting sts, there will be 1 extra st on Rows 36-38 of Lace Diamond Panel.

Work even as established until Left Front measures same number of rows as for Back to underarm, end with WS row.

Armhole shaping: Bind off 5 sts at the beginning of the next row, then decrease one st at the beginning of the next 6{9-10-12} RS rows — 46{47-50-52} sts.

Work even as established until Row 18 of 5th{5th-6th-6th} rep of Lace Diamond Panel is complete — armhole depth should measure approximately 3$\frac{1}{4}${3$\frac{3}{4}$-4$\frac{3}{4}$-5$\frac{1}{4}$}"/8.5{9.5-12-13.5} cm.

Left Front neck shaping: (Row 19 of Lace Diamond Panel) (RS): Work to last 10 sts of row, join a short second strand of yarn and bind off last 10 sts — 36{37-40-42} sts.

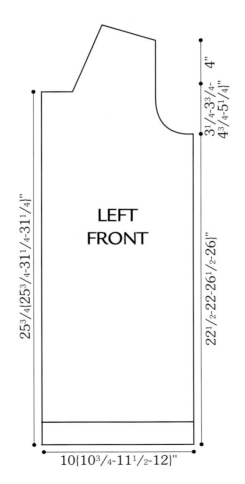

LEFT FRONT

25$\frac{3}{4}${25$\frac{3}{4}$-31$\frac{1}{4}$-31$\frac{1}{4}$}"

3$\frac{1}{4}$-3$\frac{3}{4}$- 4"
4$\frac{3}{4}$-5$\frac{1}{4}$}"

22$\frac{1}{2}$-22-26$\frac{1}{2}$-26}"

10{10$\frac{3}{4}$-11$\frac{1}{2}$-12}"

Next row (WS): With old strand, work WS row as established.

Next row (RS): Keeping in patterns, work to last 4 sts, K2 tog, P2 as established — 35{36-39-41} sts.

Next row: K2, work in patterns as established to end.

Rep last 2 rows 12{12-13-14} more times — 23{24-26-27} sts.

Keeping in patterns, even in Lace Diamond Panel if possible, work even until same number of rows have been worked as for Back to shoulder, so end with a WS row — armhole depth measures approximately $7^1/_4\{7^3/_4$-$8^3/_4$-$9^1/_4\}$"/ 18.5{19.5-22-23.5} cm.

Shoulder shaping (RS): Bind off 8{8-9-9} sts at the beginning of the next 2{3-2-3} RS rows, then 7{0-8-0} sts at beginning of next RS row.

RIGHT FRONT

With smaller needles, cast on 65{69-73-77} sts.

Row 1 (RS): K2, P1, * K1, P1; rep from * across to last 2 sts, end K2.

Row 2: P2, K1, * P1, K1; rep from * across to last 2 sts, end P2.

Rep these last 2 rows once more, increase 1 st on last WS row — 66{70-74-78} sts.

Next row (RS): K2, * P2, K2; rep from * across.

Next row: P2, * K2, P2; rep from * across.

Rep these last 2 rows until piece measures same as for Back, end with a RS row.

Next row (WS): Purl across, decrease 8 sts evenly spaced — 58{62-66-70} sts.

Change to larger needles.

Next row, set up patterns: (RS): K2 (edge sts: keep in St st), PM, work Row 1 of Cable Panel over 10 sts, PM, work Row 1 of Lace Diamond Panel over 24 sts, PM, work Row 1 of Cable Panel over 10 sts, PM, work Row 1 of Lace Column Pattern over 12{12-12-22} sts, PM (except size Small), K 0{4-8-2} (edge sts: keep in St st) — 57{61-65-69} sts.

Instructions continued on page 82.

Note: When counting sts, there will be 1 extra st on rows 36-38 of Lace Diamond Panel.

Work even as established until Right Front measures same number of rows as for Back to underarm, end with RS row.

Armhole shaping: Bind off 5 sts at the beginning of the next row, then decrease 1 st at the end of the next 6{9-10-12} RS rows — 46{47-50-52} sts.

Work even as established until Row 18 of 5th{5th-6th-6th} rep of Lace Diamond Panel is complete — armhole depth should measure approximately 3$\frac{1}{4}${3$\frac{3}{4}$-4$\frac{3}{4}$-5$\frac{1}{4}$}"/8.5{9.5-12-13.5} cm.

Right Front neck shaping: (Row 19 of Lace Diamond Panel) (RS): Bind off first 10 sts, work to end — 36{37-40-42} sts.

Next row (WS): Work WS row as established.

Next row (RS): P2, SSK, work in patterns to end — 35{36-39-41} sts.

Next row (WS): Keeping in patterns, work to last 2 sts, K2.

Rep last 2 rows 12{12-13-14} more times — 23{24-26-27} sts.

Keeping in patterns, even in Lace Diamond Panel if possible, work even until same number of rows have been worked as for Back to shoulder, so end with a RS row — armhole depth measures approximately 7$\frac{1}{4}${7$\frac{3}{4}$-8$\frac{3}{4}$-9$\frac{1}{4}$}"/ 18.5{19.5-22-23.5} cm.

Shoulder shaping (WS): Bind off 8{8-9-9} sts at the beginning of the next 2{3-2-3} WS rows, then 7{0-8-0} sts at beginning of next WS row.

SLEEVES

With larger needles, cast on 46{46-46-48} sts.

Row 1 (RS): K2{2-2-3} (edge sts: keep in St st), work in Lace Column Pattern over center 42 sts, end K2{2-2-3} (edge sts: keep in St st).

Work as established for 3 more rows, end with a WS row.

Next row, increase row (RS): K2, make 1 *(Figs. 5a & b, page 110)*, work to last 2 sts, make 1, end K2 — 48{48-48-50} sts.

Keeping in pattern, working increases into Lace Column Pattern when possible, increase 1 st at each edge every 6th row 0{2-6-10} times, every 8th row 0{11-8-5} times, then every 10th row 10{0-0-0} times for a total of 11{14-15-16} increases each side — 68{74-76-80} sts.

Work even until Sleeve measures approximately 17$\frac{1}{2}$" (44.5 cm), end with a WS row.

Cap shaping: Bind off 5 sts at the beginning of the next 2 rows — 58{64-66-70} sts.

Next row (RS): K1, SSK, work to last 3 sts, K2 tog, K1.

Next row (WS): P2, work in pattern as established to last st, end P2.

Rep these 2 rows 14{15-16-18} more times — 28{32-32-32} sts.

Bind off 2 sts at the beginning of the next 2{4-4-4} rows.

Bind off 3 sts at the beginning of the next 2 rows — 18 sts.

Bind off remaining sts.

FINISHING

Sew Fronts to Back at shoulders.

Weave sides seams *(Fig. 15, page 112)*.

Weave Sleeve seams.

Sew Sleeve caps into armholes, easing in any fullness.

Instructions continued on page 84.

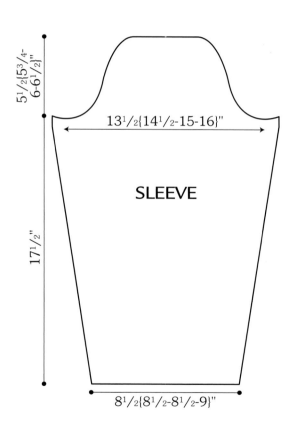

5$\frac{1}{2}${5$\frac{3}{4}$-6-6$\frac{1}{2}$}"

13$\frac{1}{2}${14$\frac{1}{2}$-15-16}"

SLEEVE

17$\frac{1}{2}$"

8$\frac{1}{2}${8$\frac{1}{2}$-8$\frac{1}{2}$-9}"

Mitered Neckline rib: With RS facing and smaller needles, starting at right Front, pick up 12 sts to corner *(Figs. 14a & b, page 112)*, then pick up 1 st in corner and mark this st, then pick up 32{34-38-40} sts to shoulder, 49{49-51-53} sts across Back neck to shoulder, then 32{34-38-40} sts to corner, then pick up 1 st in corner and mark this st, then pick up 12 sts to end — 139{143-153-159} sts.

Next row (WS): P2, K1, * P1, K1; rep from * across to last 2 sts, end P2.

Next row, decrease row (RS): K2, * K1, P1; rep from * across to 1 st before marked st, then slip the marked st tog knit-wise with the st before it, work next st as established, then pass the 2 slipped sts tog over this st; rib as established to 1 st before next marked st, then slip the marked st tog knit-wise with the st before it, work next st as established, then pass the 2 slipped sts tog over this st, rib as established to last 2 sts, end K2. Rib WS row as established, purl the marked st. Work mitered decrease at both corners every RS row.

When rib measures approximately 1" (2.5 cm), bind off in rib.

Left Seed Stitch button band: With RS facing and smaller needles, starting at Left Front neckline edge, pick up 149{151-153-155} sts evenly spaced along Left Front.

Next row (WS): P1, * K1, P1; rep from * across.

Rep this row until band measures approximately 1" (2.5 cm), then bind off in pattern.

Sew 7 buttons evenly spaced along this band.

Right Seed Stitch buttonhole band: Work same as for Left band, working 7 three-st buttonholes evenly spaced (by binding off 3 sts and casting on 3 sts on next row), opposite buttons on Left Band.

Hooded
LACE JACKET

A stand-out among hoodies, this lacy cover-up appeals to romantic souls with its allover lace and dreamy soft yarn. Roomy sleeves make it ultra-comfortable, and the hood gets a dramatic lift from its sectioned construction. Garter stitch trim provides a polished finish all around.

SIZES

To fit sizes Small{Medium-Large-Extra Large}.
Sample in size Medium.

MEASUREMENTS

Finished bust at underarm:

35{39-41-45}"/89{99-104-114.5} cm

Length from back neck:

20{20$^1/_2$-21-21$^1/_2$}"/51{52-53.5-54.5} cm

Sleeve width at upper arm:

16$^1/_4${17$^1/_2$-18$^1/_4$-19$^1/_4$}"/41.5{44.5-46.5-49} cm

Size Note: Instructions are written for size Small with sizes Medium, Large, and Extra Large in braces { }. Instructions will be easier to read if you circle all the numbers pertaining to your size. If only one number is given, it applies to all sizes.

MATERIALS

BLUE SKY ALPACAS "Dyed Cotton"

(100% Cotton; 100 grams/150 yards)

Color #626 (Stone): 7{8-9-10} hanks

Straight knitting needles, sizes 7 (4.5 mm) **and**

8 (5 mm) **or** sizes needed to obtain gauge

24" (61 cm) Circular knitting needle, size 7 (4.5 mm)

Stitch holder

$^5/_8$" (16 mm) Buttons - 6

Sewing needle and thread

Yarn needle

Instructions begin on page 90.

88

"This simple lace pattern gives new life to the ever-popular hoodie!" Deborah said. "The thick cotton yarn makes this a perfect garment for a beach cover-up, but worked in luxe mohair or cashmere (with rhinestone buttons?), this could be the perfect simple holiday sweater."

GAUGE
Over Lace Pattern using size 8 needles:
16 sts and 22 rows = 4"(10 cm).
Take time to save time, check your gauge.

PATTERN STITCHES
LACE PATTERN: Multiple of 6 sts plus 1
Rows 1, 3, and 5 (RS): K1, * YO *(Fig. 3a, page 109)*, SSK *(Figs. 11a-c, page 111)*, K1, K2 tog *(Fig. 7, page 110)*, YO, K1; rep from * across.
Row 2 AND ALL WS ROWS: Purl across.
Row 7: K2, * YO, [slip 1, K2 tog, PSSO *(Figs. 12a & b, page 112)]*, YO, K3; rep from * across to last 2 sts, end last rep K2.
Row 9: K1, * K2 tog, YO, K1, YO, SSK, K1; rep from * across.
Row 11: K2 tog, * YO, K3, YO, slip 1, K2 tog, PSSO; rep from * across to last 5 sts, YO, K3, YO, SSK.
Row 12: Purl across.
Rep Rows 1-12 for Lace Pattern.

STOCKINETTE STITCH (St st):
Any number of sts
Knit RS rows, purl WS rows.

GARTER STITCH (Garter st): Any number of sts
Knit every row.

BACK
With smaller needles, cast on 67{75-79-87} sts.

Work in Garter st for 3 rows, increase 6 sts evenly spaced across last row *(see Increases, page 110 and Increasing Evenly Across A Row, page 110)* — 73{81-85-93} sts.

Change to larger needles.

Next row (RS): K3{1-3-1} (edge sts: keep in St st), work Row 1 of Lace Pattern over center 67{79-79-91} sts, end K3{1-3-1} (edge sts: keep in St st).

Work even in pattern until piece measures approximately 13" (33 cm), end with a WS row.

Shape armholes: Bind off 2 sts at the beginning of the next 4{6-6-8} rows — 65{69-73-77} sts.

Keeping 1 edge st each side in St st, work even in pattern until armhole depth measures approximately 7{7$\frac{1}{2}$-8-8$\frac{1}{2}$}"/18{19-20.5-21.5} cm, end with a WS row.

Shape back neck and shoulders: Mark center 9 sts.

Next row (RS): Bind off 6{7-8-8} sts, work to center marked sts, join a second ball of yarn, bind off center 9 sts, work to end.

Working both sides at the same time with separate balls of yarn, bind off 6{7-8-8} sts at the beginning of the next 5{3-1-5} shoulder edges, then 0{6-7-0} sts on next 0{2-4-0} shoulder edges *(see Zeros, page 108)* AND AT THE SAME TIME, bind off 5 sts from each neck edge twice.

LEFT FRONT

With smaller needles, cast on 32{36-38-42} sts.

Work in Garter st for 3 rows, increase 3 sts evenly spaced across last row — 35{39-41-45} sts.

Change to larger needles.

Next row (RS): K3{1-3-1} (edge sts: keep in St st), work Row 1 of Lace Pattern over center 31{37-37-43} sts, end K1 (edge sts: keep in St st).

Work even in pattern until piece measures approximately 13" (33 cm), end with a WS row.

Shape armhole: Bind off 2 sts at the beginning of the next 2{3-3-4} RS rows — 31{33-35-37} sts.

Instructions continued on page 92.

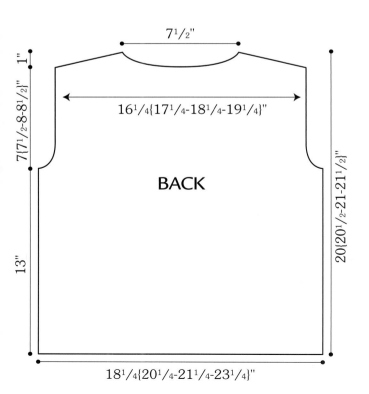

BACK

7½"

16¼{17¼-18¼-19¼}"

7{7½-8-8½}"

1"

13"

20{20½-21-21½}"

18¼{20¼-21¼-23¼}"

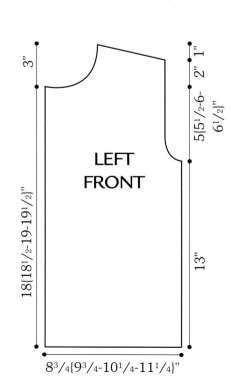

LEFT FRONT

3"

5{5½-6-6½}"

2"

1"

18{18½-19-19½}"

13"

8¾{9¾-10¼-11¼}"

Work even as established until armhole depth measures approximately 5{5$\frac{1}{2}$-6-6$\frac{1}{2}$}"/12.5{14-15-16.5} cm, end with a RS row.

Shape left front neck (WS): From neck edge at beginning of WS rows, bind off 5 sts once, then bind off 2 sts 4 times — 18{20-22-24} sts.

Work even as established until armhole measures same as Back to shoulder, end with a WS row.

Shape shoulder (RS): Bind off 6{7-8-8} sts from the beginning of the next 3{2-1-3} shoulder edges, then 0{6-7-0} sts on next 0{1-2-0} shoulder edges.

RIGHT FRONT

With smaller needles, cast on 32{36-38-42} sts.

Work in Garter st for 3 rows, increase 3 sts evenly spaced across last row — 35{39-41-45} sts.

Change to larger needles.

Next row (RS): K1 (edge sts: keep in St st), work Row 1 of Lace Pattern over center 31{37-37-43} sts, end K3{1-3-1} (edge sts: keep in St st).

Work even in pattern until piece measures approximately 13" (33 cm), end with a RS row.

Shape armhole: Bind off 2 sts at the beginning of the next 2{3-3-4} WS rows — 31{33-35-37} sts.

Work even as established until armhole depth measures approximately 5{5$\frac{1}{2}$-6-6$\frac{1}{2}$}"/12.5{14-15-16.5} cm, end with a WS row.

Shape right front neck (RS): From neck edge at beginning of RS rows, bind off 5 sts once, then bind off 2 sts 4 times — 18{20-22-24} sts.

Work even as established until armhole measures same as Back to shoulder, end with a RS row.

Shape shoulder (WS): Bind off 6{7-8-8} sts from the beginning of the next 3{2-1-3} shoulder edges, then 0{6-7-0} sts on next 0{1-2-0} shoulder edges.

SLEEVES

With smaller needles, cast on 36{36-36-42} sts.

Work in Garter st for 3 rows, increase 3 sts evenly spaced across last row — 39{39-39-45} sts.

Change to larger needles.

Next row (RS): K1 (edge sts: keep in St st), work Row 1 of Lace Pattern over center 37{37-37-43} sts, end K1 (edge sts: keep in St st).

Work even as established for 5 more rows, end with a WS row.

Next row, increase row (RS): K1, make 1 *(Figs. 5a & b, page 110)*, work in pattern to last st, make 1, end K1 — 41{41-41-47} sts.

Keeping edge sts each end in St st as established, and working increases into pattern, rep increase row every 6th {6th-4th-4th} row 6{14-6-3} more times, then every 8th{0-6th-6th } row 6{0-10-12} times — 65{69-73-77} sts.

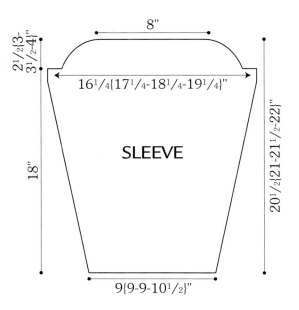

Work until Sleeve measures approximately 18" (45.5 cm), end with a WS row.

Cap shaping (RS): Bind off 2 sts at the beginning of the next 4{6-14-16} rows, then bind off 3 sts at the beginning of the next 8{8-4-4} rows — 33 sts.

Bind off remaining sts.

HOOD

Back section: With larger needles, cast on 33 sts.

Next row (RS): K1 (edge sts: keep in St st), work Row 1 of Lace Pattern over center 31 sts, end K1 (edge sts: keep in St st).

Work even until piece measures approximately 11" (28 cm), end with a WS row.

Side sections: Cable cast on 48 sts at the beginning of the next 2 rows *(Figs. 1a & b, page 109)* — 129 sts.

Keeping 1 edge st each end in St st, work even in Lace Pattern over center 127 sts until side sections above cast on sts measure 6" (15 cm).

Slip sts to st holder.

Instructions continued on page 94.

FINISHING

Sew Fronts to Back at shoulders.

Weave side seams *(Fig. 15, page 112)*.

Sew cast on edges of Hood to sides of back section.

Matching front edge of Hood to start of neck shaping on each side, sew Hood to neckline.

Trim for hood and front edges: With circular needle, starting at bottom edge of Right Front, pick up 72{74-76-78} sts to start of neck shaping *(Figs. 14a & b, page 112)*, slip 127 sts from st holder around Hood front to left end of needle and knit across, pick up 72{74-76-78} sts down Left Front edge — 271{275-279-283} sts.

Working back and forth, knit 3 rows.

Next row (RS): Work 6 buttonholes on right front, the first approximately 3" (7.5 cm) from lower edge, and the upper one ¹/₂" (12 mm) beneath neck edge, with the others evenly spaced in between; work each buttonhole as follows: K2 tog, (YO) twice, K2 tog.

Knit 4 more rows [working K1 in first YO and K1 tbl *(Fig. 2, page 109)* of second YO of buttonhole].

Bind off all sts in knit.

Sew 6 buttons on left front opposite buttonholes.

Weave Sleeve seams.

Sew Sleeve caps into armholes, easing in any fullness.

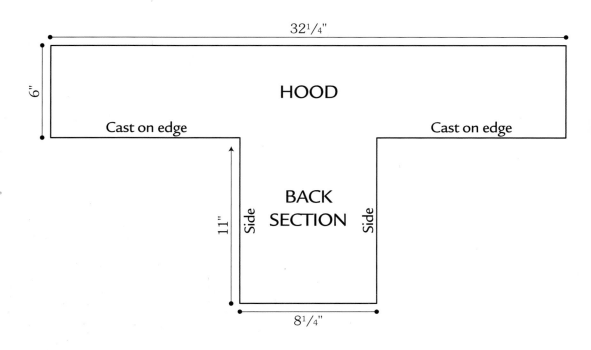

95.

$\mathscr{D}$rawstring
CARDIGAN

Feminine appeal was the goal when Deborah began sketching this sweet sweater. With a touch of glint in the yarn, it presents alluring lace patterns at every turn, from the deep V neckline to the flared peplum skirting.

SIZES

To fit sizes Small{Medium-Large-Extra Large}.
Sample in size Small.

MEASUREMENTS

Finished bust at underarm:
36{39-44-47}"/91.5{99-112-119.5} cm
Length from back neck to top of scalloped
pattern: 17{17^1/$_2$-18-18^1/$_2$}"/43{44.5-45.5-47} cm
Peplum Length: 4" (10 cm)
Sleeve width at upper arm:
14{15-16-16^3/$_4$}"/35.5{38-40.5-42.5} cm

Size Note: Instructions are written for size Small with
sizes Medium, Large, and Extra Large in braces { }.
Instructions will be easier to read if you circle all the
numbers pertaining to your size. If only one number is
given, it applies to all sizes.

MATERIALS

NASHUA HANDKNITS "Ivy"
(50% Alpaca, 45% Merino Wool, 5% Estellina;
50 grams/137 yards)
    Color #NIVY 1004 (Copper): 8{9-10-11} balls
Straight knitting needles, sizes 6 (4 mm) **and**
    8 (5 mm) **or** sizes needed to obtain gauge
24" (61 cm) Circular knitting needle, size 6 (4 mm)
Stitch markers
Yarn needle

Instructions begin on page 100.

A play on the classic ballerina wrap sweater, this cardigan is embellished with lots of lace. "The main body pattern is one I designed by inserting eyelets into traditional knitted basketweave," Deborah explained.

GAUGES

Using size 8 needles for all:
Over Lace Basketweave Pattern:
19 sts and 28 rows = 4" (10 cm).
Over Lace Panel: 17 sts = 3" (7.5 cm),
25 rows = 4" (10 cm).
Over Scalloped Pattern: 20 sts and
25 rows = 4" (10 cm).
Take time to save time, check your gauge.

PATTERN STITCHES

STOCKINETTE STITCH (St st):
Any number of sts
Knit RS rows, purl WS rows.

LACE BASKETWEAVE PATTTERN:
Multiple of 6 sts plus 2
Row 1 (RS): K1, YO *(Fig. 3a, page 109)*,
SSK *(Figs. 11a-c, page 111)*, * K2, (YO,
SSK) 2 times; rep from * across to last
5 sts, end K2, YO, SSK, K1.
Row 2: Purl across.
Rows 3 and 5: K2, * P4, K2; rep from *
across.
Rows 4 and 6: P2, * K4, P2; rep from *
across.
Row 7: K2, * [K2 tog *(Fig. 7, page 110)*,
YO] 2 times, K2; rep from * across.
Row 8: Purl across.
Rows 9 and 11: P3, * K2, P4; rep from
* across to last 5 sts, end K2, P3.
Rows 10 and 12: K3, * P2, K4; rep
from * across to last 5 sts, end P2, K3.
Rep Rows 1-12 for Lace Basketweave
Pattern.

LACE PANEL: Over 17 sts
Row 1 (RS): P1, K1, (K2 tog) 2 times,
(YO, K1) 3 times, YO, (SSK) 2 times,
K3, P1.
Row 2 AND ALL WS ROWS: K1,
P 15, K1.
Row 3: P1, (K2 tog) 2 times, YO, K1,
YO, K3, YO, K1, YO, (SSK) 2 times, K2, P1.
Row 5: P1, K3, (K2 tog) 2 times, (YO,
K1) 3 times, YO, (SSK) 2 times, K1, P1.
Row 7: P1, K2, (K2 tog) 2 times, YO,
K1, YO, K3, YO, K1, YO, (SSK) 2 times, P1.
Row 8: K1, P 15, K1.
Rep Rows 1-8 for Lace Panel.

SCALLOPED PATTERN: Multiple of
14 sts plus 1
Rows 1, 3, 5, 7, and 9 (WS): Purl
across.
Rows 2, 4, 6, 8, and 10: K1, * YO,
K3, SSK, YO, [slip 1, K2 tog, PSSO
(Figs. 12a & b, page 112)], YO, K2 tog,
K3, YO, K1; rep from * across.
Row 11: Knit across.
Row 12: Purl across.
Rep Rows 1-12 for Scalloped Pattern.

K1, P1 RIB: Odd number of sts
Row 1: P1, * K1, P1; rep from * across.
Row 2: K1, * P1, K1; rep from across.
Rep Rows 1-2 for K1, P1 Rib.

BACK

With larger needles,
cast on 78{84-96-102} sts.

Row 1 (RS): Purl across.

Row 2 (WS): K2 (edge sts: keep in St st), work in Lace Basketweave Pattern over center 74{80-92-98} sts, end K2 (edge sts: keep in St st).

Work even as established for 17 more rows, end with a WS row.

Waist shaping: Next row, increase row (RS): K2, make 1 *(Figs. 5a & b, page 110)*, work to last 2 sts, make 1, end K2 — 80{86-98-104} sts.

Working increases into pattern and keeping edge sts in St st, rep increase row every 12th{10th-10th-10th} row, 3{4-4-4} more times — 86{94-106-112} sts.

Work even as established until piece measures approximately 9 1/2" (24 cm), end with a WS row.

Armhole shaping: Bind off 5 sts at the beginning of the next 2 rows, then decrease 1 st each end of the next 5{6-10-10} RS rows as follows: SSK, work to last 2 sts, end K2 tog. Work WS rows as established, keeping 1 st each side in St st for edge — 66{72-76-82} sts.

Instructions continued on page 102.

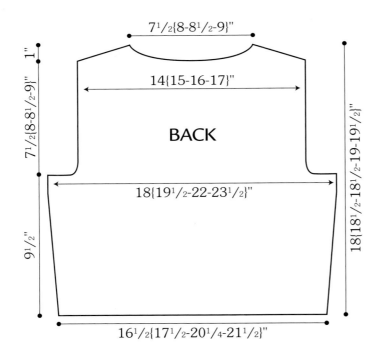

7 1/2{8-8 1/2-9}"

1"

7 1/2{8-8 1/2-9}"

14{15-16-17}"

BACK

18{18 1/2-18 1/2-19-19 1/2}"

18{19 1/2-22-23 1/2}"

9 1/2"

16 1/2{17 1/2-20 1/4-21 1/2}"

Work even as established in pattern until armhole depth measures approximately 7$\frac{1}{2}${8-8$\frac{1}{2}$-9}"/19{20.5-21.5-23} cm, end with a WS row.

Shape shoulders and back neck:
Mark center 16{18-20-22} sts.

Next row (RS): Bind off 5{6-6-7} sts, work as established to center marked sts, join a second ball of yarn and bind off center 16{18-20-22} sts, work to end of row.

Working both sides at the same time with separate balls of yarn, bind off 5{6-6-7} sts at the beginning of the next 5{3-5-3} shoulder edges, then 0{5-0-6} sts at beginning of next 2 shoulder edges *(see Zeros, page 108)* AND AT THE SAME TIME, bind off 5 sts from each neck edge twice.

LEFT FRONT
With larger needles, cast on 47{49-55-59} sts.

Row 1 (WS): Purl across.

Row 2 (RS): K2{4-4-2} (edge sts: keep in St st), PM *(see Markers, page 108)*, work Lace Basketweave Pattern over next 26{26-32-38} sts, PM, work Lace Panel over next 17 sts, PM, end K2 (edge sts: keep in St st).

Work even as established for 9 more rows, end with a WS row.

Next row, neckline decrease row (RS): Work to last st of Lace Basketweave Pattern and P2 tog tbl *(Fig. 10, page 111)* this st with the first st of Lace Panel, work as established to end — 46{48-54-58} sts. (**Note:** You will have to remove the marker before doing this and replace it afterwards).

Note: There will always be 17 sts in Lace Panel as you replace the marker.

Keeping in patterns, work neckline decrease row after 3 more rows, then alternately every 6th and 4th rows after for a total of 22{22-23-25} Front decreases AND AT THE SAME TIME, work waist shaping as for Back until piece measures same as Back to armhole, end with a WS row.

Shape armhole (RS): Keeping in patterns, continue decreases along Front neck edge, work same armhole shaping as for Back at beginning of rows — 19{21-22-24} sts.

Work as established until armhole depth measures same as for Back, end with a WS row.

Shoulder shaping (RS): Bind off 6{7-7-8} sts at the beginning of the next 2{3-2-3} RS rows, then 7{0-8-0} sts at beginning of next RS row.

Note: There are 4 more sts for shoulders on Fronts than on Back however, pieces should measure the same.

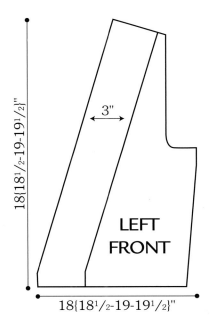

RIGHT FRONT

With larger needles, cast on 47{49-55-59} sts.

Row 1 (WS): Purl across.

Row 2 (RS): K2 (edge sts: keep in St st), PM, work Lace Panel over next 17 sts, PM, work Lace Basketweave Pattern over next 26{26-32-38} sts, PM, end K2{4-4-2} (edge sts: keep in St st).

Work even as established for 9 more rows, end with a WS row.

Next row, neckline decrease row (RS): Work to last st of Lace Panel and P2 tog *(Fig. 9, page 111)* this st with the first st of Lace Basketweave Pattern, work as established to end — 46{48-54-58} sts. (*Note:* you will have to remove the marker before doing this and replace it afterwards).

Note: There will always be 17 sts in Lace Panel as you replace the marker.

Keeping in patterns, work neckline decrease row after 3 more rows, then alternately every 6th and 4th rows after for a total of 22{22-23-25} Front decreases AND AT THE SAME TIME, work waist shaping as for Back until piece measures same as Back to armhole, end with a RS row.

Shape armhole (WS): Keeping in patterns, continue decreases along Front neck edge, work same armhole shaping as for Back at end of rows.

Instructions continued on page 104.

Work as established until armhole depth measures same as for Back, end with a RS row — 19{21-22-24} sts.

Shoulder shaping (WS): Bind off 6{7-7-8} sts at the beginning of the next 2{3-2-3} WS rows, then 7{0-8-0} sts at beginning of next WS row.

Note: There are 4 more sts for shoulders on Fronts than on Back however, pieces should measure the same.

SLEEVES

With larger needles, cast on 42{44-46-46} sts.

Row 1 (RS): Purl across.

Row 2 (WS): K2{3-4-4} (edge sts: keep in St st), work in Lace Basketweave Pattern over center 38 sts, end K2{3-4-4} (edge sts: keep in St st).

Work even as established for 12 rows.

Next row, increase row (RS): K2, make 1, work to last 2 sts, make 1, end K2 — 44{46-48-48} sts.

Keeping 2 sts each side in St st for edge sts and working increases into pattern, rep increase row every 10th{8th-8th-8th} row 2{11-8-2} more times, then every 8th{6th-6th-6th} row 10{2-6-14} times — 68{72-76-80} sts.

Work even until Sleeve measures approximately 17½" (44.5 cm), end with a WS row.

Cap shaping: Keeping in pattern as established, bind off 5 sts at the beginning of the next 2 rows — 58{62-66-70} sts.

Instructions continued on page 106.

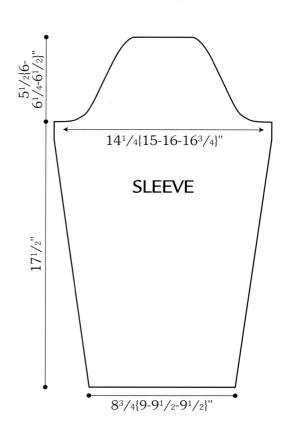

5½{6-6¼-6½}"

14¼{15-16-16¾}"

SLEEVE

17½"

8¾{9-9½-9½}"

Next row, decrease row (RS): K1, SSK, work to last 3 sts, end K2 tog, K1 — 56{60-64-68} sts.

Next row (WS): P3, work in pattern as established to last 3 sts, end P3.

Rep these 2 rows 15{17-18-20} more times — 26{26-28-28} sts.

Bind off 2 sts at the beginning of the next 4 rows — 18{18-20-20} sts.

Bind off remaining sts.

FINISHING
Weave Fronts to Back at sides *(Fig. 15, page 112)*.

Lower Peplum edge: With RS facing and circular needle, pick up 185{199-213-227} sts evenly spaced along entire lower edge *(Fig. 14b, page 112)*.

Next row (WS): P1 (edge st: knit on RS, purl on WS), work Row 1 of Scalloped Pattern over next 183{197-211-225} sts, end P1 (edge st: knit on RS, purl on WS).

Work even for 23 rows, bind off on last RS purl row (Row 12 of pattern).

Sew Fronts to Back at shoulders.

Weave Sleeve seams.

Sew Sleeve caps into armholes, easing in any fullness.

Front and neckline edge ribbing:
With circular needle, beginning at lower Right Front edge, pick up 119{121-123-125} sts along edge to shoulder *(Fig. 14a, page 112)*, then pick up 41{43-45-47} sts along Back neck edge, then pick up 119{121-123-125} sts along Left Front edge — 279{285-291-297} sts.

Work in K1, P1 rib for ¹/₂" (12 mm), then bind off in rib.

CORD: With circular needle, cast on 200{218-238-256} sts.

Bind off in purl.

Steam lightly.

Thread cord through eyelets at lower edge of Basketweave Pattern.

abbreviations

BC	back cross	mm	millimeters	RS	right side
C7B	Cable 7 Back	P	purl	Rnd(s)	Round(s)
C7F	Cable 7 Front	P2SSO	pass 2 slipped	SSK	slip, slip, knit
CC	Contrasting Color		stitches over	St st	Stockinette Stitch
cn	cable needle	PM	place marker	st(s)	stitch(es)
cm	centimeters	PSSO	pass slipped stitch over	tbl	through the back loop
K	knit	Rep	repeat	tog	together
LH	left hand	Rev St st	Reverse Stockinette	WS	wrong side
MC	Main Color		Stitch	YO	yarn over
		RH	Right Hand		

* — work instructions following * as many **more** times as indicated in addition to the first time.

( ) or **[ ]** — work enclosed instructions **as many** times as specified by the number immediately following **or** contains explanatory remarks.

work even — work without increasing or decreasing in the established pattern.

GAUGE

Exact gauge is **essential** for proper fit. Before beginning your project, make a sample swatch in the yarn and needle specified in the individual instructions. After completing the swatch, measure it, counting your stitches and rows carefully. If your swatch is larger or smaller than specified, **make another, changing needle size to get the correct gauge**. Keep trying until you find the size needles that will give you the specified gauge. Once proper gauge is obtained, measure width of garment approximately every 3" (7.5 cm) to be sure gauge remains consistent.

HINTS

As in all garments, good finishing techniques make a big difference in the quality of the piece. Do not tie knots. Always start a new ball at the beginning of a row, leaving ends long enough to weave in later. With wrong side facing, weave the needle through several stitches, then reverse the direction and weave it back through several stitches. When the ends are secure, clip them off close to the work.

ZEROS

To consolidate the length of an involved pattern, zeros are sometimes used so that all sizes can be combined. For example, increase every sixth row 5{1-0} time(s) means the first size would increase 5 times, the second size would increase once, and the largest size would do nothing.

MARKERS

As a convenience to you, we have used markers to help distinguish the beginning of a pattern, round, or stitch. Place markers as instructed. You may use purchased markers or tie a length of contrasting color yarn around the needle. When you reach a marker on each row or round, slip it from the left needle to the right needle; remove it when no longer needed.

Yarn Weight Symbol & Names	LACE 0	SUPER FINE 1	FINE 2	LIGHT 3	MEDIUM 4	BULKY 5	SUPER BULKY 6
Type of Yarns in Category	Fingering, size 10 crochet thread	Sock, Fingering, Baby	Sport, Baby	DK, Light Worsted	Worsted, Afghan, Aran	Chunky, Craft, Rug	Bulky, Roving
Knit Gauge Range* in Stockinette St to 4" (10 cm)	33-40** sts	27-32 sts	23-26 sts	21-24 sts	16-20 sts	12-15 sts	6-11 sts
Advised Needle Size Range	000-1	1 to 3	3 to 5	5 to 7	7 to 9	9 to 11	11 and larger

*GUIDELINES ONLY: The chart above reflects the most commonly used gauges and needle sizes for specific yarn categories.

** Lace weight yarns are usually knitted on larger needles to create lacy openwork patterns. Accordingly, a gauge range is difficult to determine. Always follow the gauge stated in your pattern.

KNIT TERMINOLOGY	
UNITED STATES	INTERNATIONAL
gauge =	tension
bind off =	cast off
yarn over (YO) =	yarn forward (yfwd) **or** yarn around needle (yrn)

KNITTING NEEDLES																
U.S.	0	1	2	3	4	5	6	7	8	9	10	10½	11	13	15	17
U.K.	13	12	11	10	9	8	7	6	5	4	3	2	1	00	000	---
Metric - mm	2	2.25	2.75	3.25	3.5	3.75	4	4.5	5	5.5	6	6.5	8	9	10	12.75

■□□□ BEGINNER	Projects for first-time knitters using basic knit and purl stitches. Minimal shaping.
■■□□ EASY	Projects using basic stitches, repetitive stitch patterns, simple color changes, and simple shaping and finishing.
■■■□ INTERMEDIATE	Projects with a variety of stitches, such as basic cables and lace, simple intarsia, double-pointed needles and knitting in the round needle techniques, mid-level shaping and finishing.
■■■■ EXPERIENCED	Projects using advanced techniques and stitches, such as short rows, fair isle, more intricate intarsia, cables, lace patterns, and numerous color changes.

CABLE CAST ON

Insert the right needle **between** the first and second stitch on the left needle, yarn over and pull loop through *(Fig. 1a)*, insert the left needle into the loop just worked from **front** to **back** and slip the loop onto the left needle *(Fig. 1b)*. Repeat for required number of stitches.

Fig. 1a

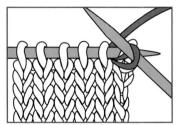

Fig. 1b

KNIT THROUGH THE BACK LOOP
(abbreviated K tbl)

Insert the right needle into the **back** of next stitch from **front** to **back** *(Fig. 2)*, then **knit** the stitch.

Fig. 2

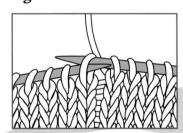

YARN OVERS

A yarn over *(abbreviated YO)* is simply placing the yarn over the right needle creating an extra stitch. Since the yarn over produces a hole in the knit fabric, it is used for a lacy effect. On the row following a yarn over, you must be careful to keep it on the needle and treat it as a stitch by knitting or purling it as instructed.

To make a yarn over, you'll loop the yarn over the needle like you would to knit or purl a stitch, bringing it either to the front or the back of the piece so that it'll be ready to work the next stitch, creating a new stitch on the needle as follows:

After a knit stitch, before a knit stitch
Bring the yarn forward **between** the needles, then back **over** the top of the right hand needle, so that it is now in position to knit the next stitch *(Fig. 3a)*.

After a purl stitch, before a purl stitch
Take yarn **over** the right hand needle to the back, then forward **under** it, so that it is now in position to purl the next stitch *(Fig. 3b)*.

After a knit stitch, before a purl stitch
Bring yarn forward **between** the needles, then back **over** the top of the right hand needle and forward **between** the needles again, so that it is now in position to purl the next stitch *(Fig. 3c)*.

After a purl stitch, before a knit stitch
Take yarn **over** right hand needle to the back, so that it is now in position to knit the next stitch *(Fig. 3d)*.

Fig. 3a

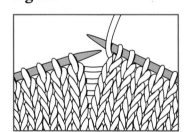

Fig. 3b

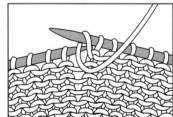

Fig. 3c

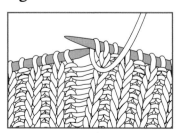

Fig. 3d

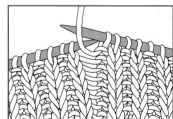

INCREASES
BAR INCREASE
Knit the next stitch but do **not** slip the old stitch off the left needle **(Fig. 4a)**. Insert the right needle into the **back** loop of the **same** stitch and knit it **(Fig. 4b)**, then slip the old stitch off the left needle.

Fig. 4a

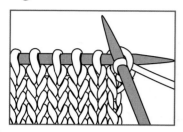

Fig. 4b

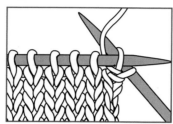

MAKE 1
Insert the **left** needle under the horizontal strand between the stitches from the front **(Fig. 5a)**. Then knit into the **back** of the strand **(Fig. 5b)**.

Fig. 5a

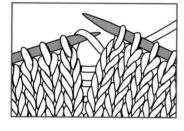

Fig. 5b

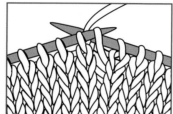

MAKE 1 PURLWISE
Insert the **left** needle under the horizontal strand between the stitches from the **back (Fig. 6)**. Then purl into the **front** of the strand.

Fig. 6

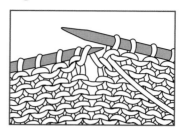

INCREASING OR DECREASING EVENLY ACROSS A ROW
Add one to the number of increases/decreases required and divide that number into the number of stitches on the needle. Subtract one from the result and the new number is the approximate number of stitches to be worked between each increase/decrease. Adjust the number as needed.

DECREASES
KNIT 2 TOGETHER *(abbreviated K2 tog)*
Insert the right needle into the **front** of the first two stitches on the left needle as if to **knit (Fig. 7)**, then **knit** them together as if they were one stitch.

Fig. 7

KNIT 3 TOGETHER *(abbreviated K3 tog)*

Insert the right needle into the **front** of the first three stitches on the left needle as if to **knit** *(Fig. 8)*, then **knit** them together as if they were one stitch.

Fig. 8

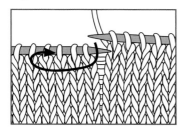

PURL 2 TOGETHER *(abbreviated P2 tog)*

Insert the right needle into the **front** of the first two stitches on the left needle as if to **purl** *(Fig. 9)*, then **purl** them together as if they were one stitch.

Fig. 9

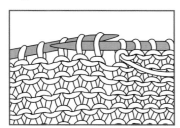

PURL 2 TOGETHER THROUGH THE BACK LOOP *(abbreviated P2 tog tbl)*

Insert the right needle into the **back** of both stitches from **back** to **front** *(Fig. 10)*, then **purl** them together.

Fig. 10

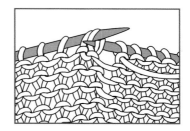

SLIP, SLIP, KNIT *(abbreviated SSK)*

Separately slip two stitches as if to **knit** *(Fig. 11a)*. Insert the **left** needle into the **front** of both slipped stitches *(Fig. 11b)* and then **knit** them together as if they were one stitch *(Fig. 11c)*.

Fig. 11a

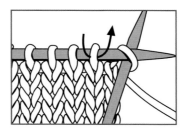

Fig. 11b

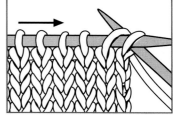

Fig. 11c

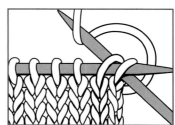

SLIP 1, KNIT 2 TOGETHER, PASS SLIPPED STITCH OVER (abbreviated slip 1, K2 tog, PSSO)

Slip one stitch as if to **knit (Fig. 12a)**, then knit the next two stitches together **(Fig. 7, page 110)**. With the left needle, bring the slipped stitch over the stitch just made **(Fig. 12b)** and off the needle.

Fig. 12a

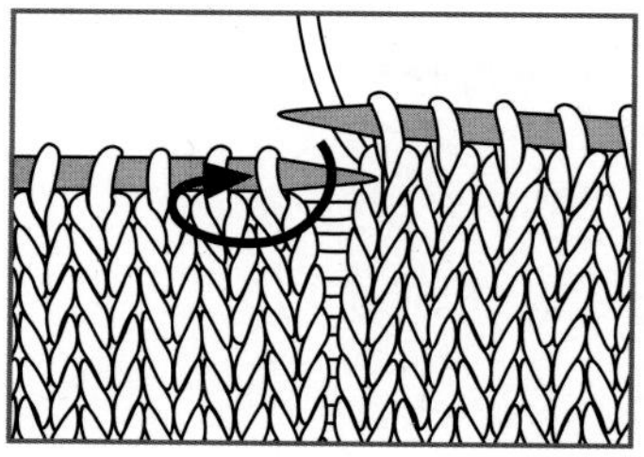

Fig. 12b

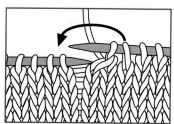

SLIP 2, KNIT 1, PASS 2 SLIPPED STITCHES OVER (abbreviated slip 2, K1, P2SSO)

Slip two stitches together as if to **knit (Fig. 13a)**, then knit the next stitch. With the left needle, bring both slipped stitches over the knit stitch **(Fig. 13b)** and off the needle.

Fig. 13a

Fig. 13b

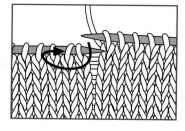

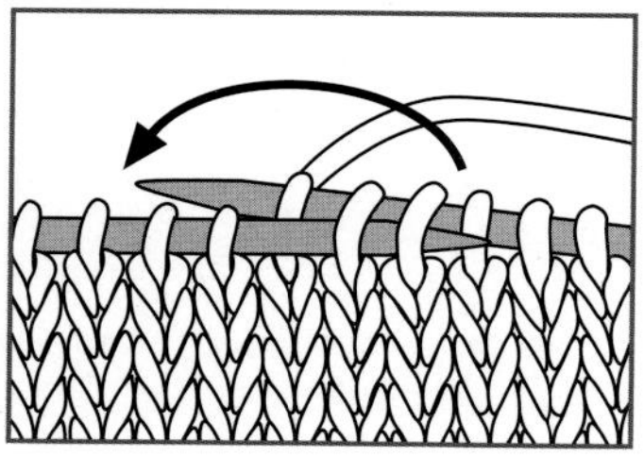

PICKING UP STITCHES

When instructed to pick up stitches, insert the needle from the **front** to the **back** under two strands at the edge of the worked piece **(Figs. 14a & b)**. Put the yarn around the needle as if to **knit**, then bring the needle with the yarn back through the stitch to the RS, resulting in a stitch on the needle.

Repeat this along the edge, picking up the required number of stitches.

A crochet hook may be helpful to pull yarn through.

Fig. 14a

Fig. 14b

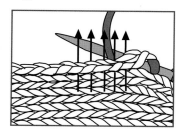
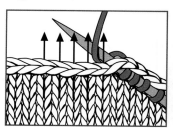

WEAVING SEAMS

With the **right** side of both pieces facing you and edges even, sew through both sides once to secure the seam. Insert the needle under the bar **between** the first and second stitches on the row and pull the yarn through **(Fig. 15)**. Insert the needle under the next bar on the second side. Repeat from side to side, being careful to match rows. If the edges are different lengths, it may be necessary to insert the needle under two bars at one edge.

Fig. 15

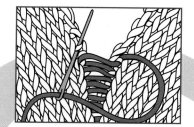